For Daron Mueller
Thank you for all your support!

LOOKING BACK
AT THE COLD WAR

30 Veterans and a
Patrol Plane Commander Remember

Don Stanton
19 Nov 18
http://skyblueThoughts.com

WingSpan Press

Published in the United States and the United Kingdom
by WingSpan Press, Livermore, CA

The WingSpan name, logo and colophon are the trademarks of WingSpan Publishing.

ISBN 978-1-59594-623-2 (pbk.)
ISBN 978-1-59594-936-3 (ebk.)

First edition 2018

Printed in the United States of America

www.wingspanpress.com

Publisher's Cataloging-in-Publication Data

Names: Stanton, Don, 1950- author.
Title: Looking back at the Cold War : 30 veterans and a patrol plane commander remember / Don Stanton.
Description: Livermore, CA : Wingspan Press, 2018.
Identifiers: LCCN 2018942108 | ISBN 978-1-59594-623-2 (pbk.) | ISBN 978-1-59594-623-2 (ebook)
Subjects: LCSH: Cold War--History. | United States--Foreign rela-tions--Soviet Union. | Soviet Union--Foreign relations--United States. | World politics--1945-1989. | Great powers--History--20th century. | Military history--20th century. | BISAC: HISTORY / Modern / 20th Century. | HISTORY / Russia & the Former Soviet Union. | HISTORY / Military / General.
Classification: LCC D840 .S73 2018 (print) | LCC D840 (ebook) | DDC 909.82/5--dc23.

Cover: *GNC 4N* General Navigation and Planning Chart. *DCS photo*

1 2 3 4 5 6 7 8 9 10

I enjoyed reading Don Stanton's interesting portrayal of the Cold War which consumed so much capital and so many American lives over four decades. He conveys our experience, especially that of the U.S. Navy, in intimate terms by providing anecdotes of many "Cold War Warriors" who were fully involved to the point of actual combat. I've known Don Stanton for over 20 years, since he served as a regular speaker at our retirement community, where he fascinated us with the breadth of his knowledge about world, national and local events of the day.

Rear Admiral B. C. "Mike" McCaffree Jr., USN (Retired)

As a former Air Force fighter pilot, I greatly enjoyed reading Don Stanton's insightful overview of the Cold War--it brought back memories of those complex years and how much was on the line. I believe It is especially important now that we continue to remember those who served during those dangerous times, especially those heroes who died for their countries. I strongly recommend this book for anyone who lived these times or wants to learn more about the service and sacrifices of these Cold Warriors. There are many lessons-learned from these times which can help us today in our increasingly uncertain and dangerous world.

Lieutenant Colonel Mike Donatelli, USAF (Retired)

Exhilarating read! I especially liked the Sigonella part. Great historical document describing the comradery and personal dedication of P-3 aircrews during the cold war. Felt like I was back on the flightline. This is a keeper!

Captain Tim Davison, USN (Retired)

FOREWORD

By former Fighter Weapons School instructor Mike Donatelli

I greatly enjoyed reading Don Stanton's insightful overview of the Cold War--it brought back memories of those complex years and how much was on the line.

I believe It is especially important now that we continue to remember those who served during those dangerous times, especially those heroes who died for their countries.

After graduating from the US Air Force Academy in 1979 during the height of the Cold War, I flew A-10 *Warthogs* at RAF Bentwaters UK where our job was to potentially fly against massed Soviet armor formations in the event of attack.

In 1984, I graduated from the USAF *Fighter Weapons School* at Nellis AFB and after another year in NATO, returned to Nellis, where I instructed in the Weapons School, and helped develop low intensity conflict tactics for the A-10 that were eventually employed during *Gulf War I.* At Nellis, we were constantly working to increase our tactical advantage over Soviet Integrated Air Defense Systems (IADS), Soviet armor, and Soviet fighter aircraft. Later I transitioned to the Wisconsin Air National Guard and flew A-10s and F-16s, including night missions over Panama in 1989 and flights over Northern Iraq in Operation Northern Watch in 1998.

Don and I flew together and worked on strategic planning and legislative efforts for the pilots at Delta Air Lines. As a former Delta Pilots Master Executive Council Chairman, we found his broad background and knowledge base invaluable and collaborated over many years.

Don provides unique perspectives and includes many insightful stories from veterans who served in a myriad of posts from the

1950s through the 1980s. I especially liked the Cold War Primer and photos which illustrate the massive political, economic, military, and civic commitments of many countries during the Cold War.

I strongly recommend this book for anyone who lived these times or wants to learn more about the service and sacrifices of these Cold Warriors. There are many lessons-learned from these times which can help us today in our increasingly uncertain and dangerous world.

Bravo Zulu Commander Stanton!

Mike Donatelli, Lieutenant Colonel USAF (Ret.)
Chicago, Illinois
March 2018

DEDICATION

Dedicated to the memories of

CPL Bob Schampier USMC (1968 Combined Action Platoon Bravo-1, 2nd Combined Action Group III MAF, Hoa Phu Quang Nam Province RVN)

Capt. Barry Applebee (1972 306th Bomb Wing B-52)

LT Mike Hayes (1978 VP-23 P-3)

LCDR Bob Moseley (1983 VP-1 P-3)

AMSC JT Clark (1985 VQ-1 EA-3B)

and all those who gave their lives, on both sides, while serving on Cold War operations.

---

[1] *Unit patches from USMC Combined Action Program; US Navy VP-23 and VQ-1*

"Eternal Father, strong to save,
Whose arm hath bound the restless wave,
Who bid'st the mighty ocean deep
Its own appointed limits keep;
Oh, hear us when we cry to Thee,
For those in peril on the sea!

Lord, guard and guide the men who fly
Through the great spaces in the sky.
Be with them always in the air,
In darkening storms or sunlight fair;
Oh, hear us when we lift our prayer,
For those in peril in the air!"[2]

from the Navy Hymn

---

[2] *Eternal Father-the Navy Hymn*, Department of the Navy; aviation verse by Mary
   C. D. Hamilton *"Lord Guard and Guide the Men Who Fly"* 1915

PREFACE

This book is an attempt to paint a brief political-military overview of the complex Cold War years, highlighted by Veteran's stories of their individual experiences. Veterans and civilians served in a myriad of positions which were vital to national defense efforts. Millions served on both sides of the Superpower confrontation and fought in wars, stood watches and manned bases, remote outposts, ships, submarines, aircraft, and missile installations and supported defense establishments.

The Cold War affected not just those serving in the military and defense industries, but also had wide-ranging effects on families and communities. Women had to adapt to separations and bore the brunt of single-handedly running families during long deployments and Temporary Duties (TDYs), moving every few years, living on remote bases--and children growing up in these conditions developed resilience early.

From 1947 through 1991, the Cold War touched millions across the world in different ways. In America, there was a near universal fear of the spread of Communism, a willingness to serve in the military, and the need to pay increased taxes to support massive defense spending. I was born in 1950 and looking back, my early memories of the Cold War range from being taught to *"duck and cover"* in elementary school to hearing returning men talk serving in faraway places like Germany, Japan, Thailand, and Korea.

While working on this book, I had wonderful experiences communicating with many people who had served around the world and lived through these difficult times and I became increasingly aware of the complexity and multi-dimensional nature of the Cold War. The long Superpower competition had many different deep effects around the world, ranging from military and civilian service, taxes and budgets, to civil defense, industrial, scientific, and social mobilization.

While this book could have been edited down, I chose to include detailed Veteran's stories told in their own words, interspersed with supporting political-military background information to portray the labyrinth of the chaotic Cold War years. The more stories I heard and read, the more complicated and multi-dimensional the Cold War became and I recognize that I have only scratched the surface of those tense times.

While memories of the Cold War and those who served during it have faded, it is especially important now that we now look back at these critical times to help inform our present realities.

Don Stanton
Arvada, Colorado

ACKNOWLEDGEMENTS

This book is the result of the generosity of Veterans who told their stories and openly shared their photographs and memories. I had the honor and wonderful experience of communicating with many individuals who served in a wide range of demanding roles around the world during difficult times in the Cold War years. I appreciated the Veterans' humility and candor as they related their vital and often dangerous Service experiences.

I am grateful to each of you for taking the time to share your important Service stories; my sincere thanks to you all!

Navy: Joe Brundage, Jim Cole, Ted Klapka, Ken Klocek, Herrick K. Lidstone Jr, B.C. (Mike) McCaffree Jr, John McMahon, Charles Morris, Mike Murphy, Mike Olenick, Daryl Phillippi, Roger Stambaugh, Steve Thiel, Warren Tisdale, Ron Wheeler

Air Force: Dino Atsalis, Mike Donatelli, Hal Donahue, Steve Raymond, Steve Walsworth

Army: Bob Evans, John Morrison, Ralph Timmons

The Lao-Hmong Special Guerilla Unit

Coast Guard Michael Cowan

Royal Canadian Air Force Norm Donovan

NASA Jet Propulsion Lab Rich Passamaneck

Department of Energy National Labs Hank Zeile

*My great thanks to Ellen Stanton for her support and ideas and to our friends, **Bob Chaloux Lieutenant Colonel Canadian Army***

*(Retired) and former Navy TACCO **Warren Tisdale**, who helped with their thoughtful reviews, suggestions, and encouragement over the past years. My appreciation to WingSpan Publishing **Editor David Collins** for his professional expertise in making this book a reality. And in memory of **Marjorie Lemka Stanton** who taught us all to love books and reading, but didn't get to finish her book.*

CONTENTS

Guide to Abbreviations and Terms

ABM   Anti-Ballistic Missile defense

Admirals Revolt 1949 Navy defiance of Truman Administration's deep cuts to Navy programs

AEC   Atomic Energy Commission

ADIZ   Air Defense Identification Zone

AFB   Air Force Base

AGI   Auxiliary General Intelligence Soviet trawlers

AOCS Aviation Officer Candidate School

ALCM Air-Launched Cruise Missile

ASW   Anti-Submarine Warfare

Atomic bomb   Nuclear fission bomb

AW   **Aviation Anti-Submarine Warfare Operator**

Bandung Conference   1955 conference of African and Asian developing countries

Berlin Airlift 1948-49 Allied supply of Berlin after Soviets blockaded the city

CAC   Combat Air Crew

CAP   Marine Combined Action Platoon

CFB   Canadian Forces Base

CG   Cruiser Guided missile

Chrome Dome   Air Force B-52 nuclear-armed bombers airborne around the clock

CINCLANT   Commander in Chief, Atlantic Fleet

DD   Destroyer

Data Link Bursts of information shared quickly between aircraft and other computers

Dead Hand *"Systema Perimetr"* nuclear control system to enable Soviet Second Strike-back capability

Decapitation Strike A nuclear attack which wipes out leadership and command and control ability to respond

DEW Line Distant Early Warning radar stations

Dien Bien Phu 1954 Viet Minh defeat of French forces

Domino theory If communists took over a country, then neighboring countries would fall

EA-3B Large Navy Electronic Intercept carrier-borne aircraft

EC-121 (WV-2) Early Warning & Control Air Force aircraft (Navy equivalent *Willie Victor*-2)

ELINT Electronic Intelligence

EMCON Emission Control

FCDA Federal Civil Defense Administration

F/E Patrol plane Flight Engineer

FLIR Forward Looking Infrared Radar

Fulda Gap German lowlands through which a potential Soviet tank attack would come

GCA Ground Controlled Approach

GIUK Gap Greenland Iceland UK gaps through which Soviet submarines transited

Hueys Bell UH-1 *Iroquois* utility helicopters used extensively in Vietnam

Hydrogen bomb Thermonuclear fusion bomb

ICBM Intercontinental Ballistic Missile

IFT In Flight Technician

INF Treaty Intermediate-Range Nuclear Forces Treaty

INS Inertial Navigation System

IADS Integrated Air Defense System

JPL   NASA's Caltech Jet Propulsion Laboratory

LCU   Landing Craft Utility

LCM-8 Landing Craft Mechanized, Mark 8

LPD   Landing Platform Dock

LPH   Landing Pad Helicopter

LSD   Landing Ship Dock

LRRPs Long Range Reconnaissance Patrols

LZ   Landing Zone

MACV Military Assistance Command Vietnam

MAD   Magnetic Anomaly Detection run by Sensor 3

MAD   Mutually Assured Destruction

Mercury Seven The first 7 American astronauts selected in 1959 for the manned space program

MiG-15 Mikoyan-Gurevich 15 fighter

MIRV   Multiple Independently Target Re-entry Vehicle

NAF   Naval Air Facility

NAS   Naval Air Station

NATO North Atlantic Treaty Organization

NAVCOM   Junior NFO in charge of navigation, inertials, communications, data link

NFO   Naval Flight Officer

NLF   National Liberation Front

NORAD   North American Air Defense Command

Nuclear Deterrence Maintaining nuclear capabilities to prevent an attack

Nuclear Triad   Nuclear-armed bombers, Intercontinental Ballistic Missiles, and Submarine-Launched Ballistic Missiles

NVA   North Vietnamese Army

OMGs   Soviet Army Operational Maneuver Groups

Ordnanceman   Crewman on an ASW aircraft responsible for sonobuoys and weapons

P-2, P-3 Navy patrol planes

Partial Test Ban Treaty 1963 treaty which prohibited all nuclear tests except for those conducted underground

PBR Patrol Boat Riverine

POW Prisoner of War

PPC Patrol Plane Commander

PPTN Patrol Plane Tactical Navigator

RAF British Royal Air Force

RIF Reductions In Force

Rigging ships Flying low near ships to photograph and gather intelligence

RIO Radar Intercept Officer back-seater

RB-47 Air Force Reconnaissance Bomber-47

RCAF Royal Canadian Air Force

ROTC Reserve Officer Training Corps

SAC Strategic Air Command

SALT Strategic Arms Limitation Talks

SAM Surface-to-Air Missile

SDI Strategic Defense Initiative

Sensor 1 and 2 Airborne Acoustic sensor operators

Sensor 3 Airborne Non-acoustic operator (Radar, MAD, EW, FLIR etc.)

SERE Survival Evasion Resistance and Escape training

SGU Special Guerilla Unit

SIOP Single Integrated Operational Plan

SLBM Submarine-Launched Ballistic Missile

SEATO South East Asian Treaty Organization

Sonobuoys About 3-foot long tubes dropped from ASW aircraft; deploys a variable length "string" with hydrophone sensor which provides acoustic information

Sputnik First successful satellite-- launched by the Soviets in 1957

SRF Soviet Strategic Rocket Forces

SSN Submarine Nuclear-powered fast attack

SSBN Submarine Ballistic missile Nuclear-powered

Suez Crisis 1957 Britain, France, and Israel conspired to retake the Suez Canal, seized by Egypt

SUS Sound Underwater Signal

TACCO Tactical Coordinator (Senior NFO)

Tet January 1968 New Year Offensive across South Vietnam by North Vietnamese Army and Viet Cong

TOC Tactical Operations Center

Toshiba-Kongsberg scandal Japanese and Norwegian companies illegally exported numerical controlled 9-axis milling machines to the Soviets enabling them to mill smoother complex curves on submarine propellers

U-2 high altitude reconnaissance single-engine aircraft

UHF Ultra High Frequency radio

UNREP Navy Underway Replenishment of ships

USSR Union of Soviet Socialist Republics; in Russian **CCCP** Союз Сове́тских Социалисти́ческих Респу́блик

V bombers Royal Air Force *Valiant, Vulcan, Victor* bombers

VC Viet Cong guerrillas

VERTREP Navy helicopter Vertical Replenishment of ships

VHF Very High Frequency

VP Fixed-wing Patrol squadron

VQ Fleet Reconnaissance squadron

Warsaw Pact 1955 Soviet partnership with 7 Eastern and Central European satellite countries

PART I
Cold War Background

Berlin 1961 Soviet tank stand-off at Checkpoint Charlie *CIA*

Introduction
Renewed Tensions with Old Adversaries

It has become increasingly evident that many people have either forgotten or don't know about the 44 tense years of the Cold War and the many sacrifices made by personnel and their families on both sides of the long superpower confrontations. *I believe that now it is especially important to relook at the Cold War to put the current times in perspective and to prepare for the future. This book is an effort to paint an overview of these times with a brief Cold War primer of key events, Veterans' stories in their own words, and details of long-range anti-submarine warfare (ASW) patrol operations in Iceland and Sicily.*

Over the past few years we have **entered an era of renewed tensions with our old adversaries from the Cold War;** we are facing Russian, Chinese, and North Korean challenges in cyberspace, military, economic, and political arenas. Sadly, many Americans of all ages, including some senior leaders, have forgotten or are unaware of the significant events and sacrifices in blood and treasure made by generations of Americans, NATO, Allies--and by our adversaries--during the Cold War.

The Soviet Union brutally took-over Eastern Europe after World War II ended and Communism was spreading quickly in Greece, Italy, and France. **For many, the long** *Cold War* **began in 1947 with the** *Truman Doctrine* **to contain Communism and ended with the disintegration of the Soviet Union in 1991.** However, others assert that a form of Cold War had existed between the US and the Union of Soviet Socialist Republics (USSR formed in 1922) before World War II and that our marriage of convenience with Stalin in WWII was just a brief interlude. Historian John Lewis Gaddis notes that *"It's difficult to say precisely when the Cold War began."*[3]

---

[3] John Lewis Gaddis, *The Cold War: A New History,* New York, The Penguin Press, 2005 p.27.

While this era has faded and the sacrifices of many thousands of service personnel (on both sides) and their families may have been forgotten, we should relook at the Cold War and its lessons which can help inform us as we have now entered an era of renewed tensions with our old adversaries from the Cold War.

The Cold War dominated world events for more than four decades. It was an all-out competitive struggle on political, military, scientific, and economic fronts by the US and our allies to contain communist expansion. The Cold War included military and civil defense, massive industrial mobilization, intelligence gathering, espionage, and many deadly confrontations around the world punctuated by deadly conflicts in Korea, Berlin, Cuba. Laos, Vietnam, Angola, Congo, Central America, and other places) which killed and displaced millions of from many countries.

Many trillions of dollars were spent during the Cold War as millions of Americans and Allies --and our Soviet and Warsaw Pact counterparts served, fought in wars, stood watches, and manned bases, remote outposts, ships, submarines, aircraft, and missile installations to maintain a constant vigil around the world...and thousands were killed or injured. In a 1953 speech, President Eisenhower stated, "This new (Soviet Secretary Khrushchev) leadership confronts a free world aroused, as rarely in its history, by the will to stay free. **The free world knows, out of the bitter wisdom of experience, that vigilance and sacrifice are the price of liberty."** [4]

Looking back at the many incidents and crises of the Cold War, it is amazing that both the United States and the Soviet Union managed to stabilize their superpower stand-off and maintain controls to survive many tense events which had the potential to escalate into nuclear war. **It is a tribute to the professionals on both sides that a tense peace was maintained over forty dangerous years.**

Every day and night throughout the Cold War, Air Force crews were flying reconnaissance and deterrence missions and Navy crews were on patrol, tracking and gathering intelligence on Soviet submarines and ships. As I built this book and reached-out

---

[4]   President Dwight D. Eisenhower, *The Chance for Peace Speech* to the *American Society of Newspaper Editors,* April 16, 1953

to veterans, **I was honored and thankful to have so many wonderful experiences talking with many veterans from different Services who shared their personal stories from the 1950s through the 1980s.**

I enjoyed connecting with many P-2 and P-3 veterans who participated in a wide range of patrol activities ranging from Navy support for Vietnam to the vast American and Allied Navies' ASW (Anti-Submarine Warfare) efforts to locate and track (and potentially destroy in the event of war) Soviet submarines in the Pacific, Atlantic, and Mediterranean. In the 1970s, I served on P-3Cs which were the Navy's first airborne ASW digital computer platform with an early data link capability, "track ball" (mouse), and other new technologies eventually including touch screens.

VP (fixed-wing patrol) Losses in "peacetime" during the Cold War Crews, families, and marriages were strained by steady deployments. During my first tour **1976-79, five P-3s were lost from VP-11, 23, 8, 22 and VP-9** (ditched in North Pacific and most of the crew rescued by a Russian ship (see *The Rescue of Alfa Foxtrot 586* by Andrew C.A. Jampoler).[5] From 1980-1983 another **20 died on two P-3s from VP-50 and VP-1. Over 50 crewmen died or were injured** in these very different mishaps.

These were highly-trained volunteers from all over the United States who had stepped-up to serve their country during the Cold War *and many still remain lost at sea*. **We should not forget the unheralded sacrifices and service of those on both sides during the long Cold War.**

Renewed Tensions with Old Adversaries In December 2017, the Australian Air Force tracked Russian TU-95 Bear bomber flights from Indonesia, in 2016 the **Russians** secretly shipped weapons and advisors to the island nation of Fiji, and in 2014 Russian ships operated near Australia highlighting their expanded presence in the Asia-Pacific region. [6]

Over the past several years the Western Allies have become increasingly engaged in in countering old adversaries with the development and redeployment of military, cyber, intelligence, and surveillance assets at great costs. Relooking at the experiences

---

[5] http://www.orneveien.org/adak/contributors/jampoler/

[6] Knaus, C. (2017), *Australian Air Force put on alert after Russian long-range bombers heads south, The Guardian,* December 30, 2017, pp. 1-2

of the past and lessons-learned can help us as we enter an era of renewed tensions with our old Cold War adversaries, in Cyberspace, Ukraine, Syria, Iran, Afghanistan, North Korea, the Pacific, the South China, Baltic and Black Seas, and elsewhere.

Our new reality includes a troubling spectrum of recent political, military, and economic events such as Russia's invasion of Crimea and later Eastern Ukraine in 2014, cooperation with Iran, and the supplying arms to the Taliban and Syria.[7] In 2018, former Russian agents were tracked down and killed in the United Kingdom, opposition leaders including Alexei Navalny were arrested, and in 2015 former Vice Premier Boris Nemtsov was assassinated within sight of the Kremlin. There has also been a steady increase in dangerous incidents involving Soviet aircraft flying dangerously close to Navy and Air Force aircraft in Syria, the Baltic Sea, Black Sea, and the Pacific.

Vladimir Putin has aggressively led a resurgent and aggressive Russia and has rapidly built-up military, cyber, and intelligence capabilities including active measures to interfere in European elections and the US 2016 election and extensive infiltration of social media necessitating increased US and Allied resources and heightened vigilance. American troops have been training with Eastern European, Baltic, and Asian counterparts and are reapplying lessons-learned from the Cold War years.[8]

Russia has rapidly developed new generations of weapons systems, is providing support for North Korea, and is collaborating with China on developing new attack submarines. By 2020, the Chinese Peoples Liberation Army (PLA) Navy will have over 80 submarines compared with the US' 30 subs in the region.

China has rapidly expanded its military and intelligence capabilities, executed over 12 alleged CIA operatives[9] between 2010 and 2012, has shown an increasingly aggressive stance. China claimed most the South China sea with it controversial **"9 dash line." has built island bases in the South China Sea**, has imposed

---

[7] Carlotta Gall, *Iran Flexes in Afghanistan As US Presence Wanes, The New York Times,* August 6,2017, p.1

[8] Eric Schmitt, US Troops Train in Eastern Europe to Echoes of the Cold War, *The New York Times,* August 6, 2017, P.1

[9] Mazetti-Goldman-Schmidt-Apuzzo, *Killing CIA Informants, China crippled U.S. Spying Operations, The New York Times,* May 20, 2017

an ADIZ (Air Defense Identification Zone), and directed fighters to buzz Air Force WC-135, Navy EP-3 and P-8 aircraft.

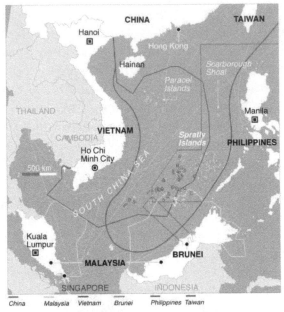

China's *9 Dash Line* claims *Voice of America*

Over several decades, China has engaged in extensive and sophisticated efforts to steal technologies to enhance their military and commercial capabilities. In 2008, American citizen and Chinese agent Tai Shen Kuo was sentenced for stealing Defense Department information and in 2014 the US indicted five Chinese military officers for stealing commercial technologies.

By 2020, the Chinese Peoples Liberation Army (PLA) Navy will have **over 80 submarines** compared with US' 30 subs in the Asia-Pacific area. **China and Russia are collaborating on developing new attack submarines and providing support for North Korea.**

North Korea has worked to miniaturize nuclear warheads and has tested several missiles which now threaten the US. Los Angeles and Ventura County, California are leading efforts to build civil defense response and education efforts for potential nuclear incidents.

To meet these rising threats and secure our nation's future, **we need to remember lessons from the Cold War such as** cherishing our allies, building-up regional and global allian-ces, upgrading civil defense programs, not entering into wars without a defined exit strategy (Vietnam and Iraq), and not encouraging uprisings which we cannot follow-through on (Hungary). We need more military and civilian leaders who serve selflessly and have experience in complex global issues, knowledge of regional histories and cultures, and are familitar with hard languages like Russian, Chinese, Arabic, and Farsi.

Chapter I
Military Service, the Draft, and
the Cold War Remembered

From 1947 through 1991, the Cold War touched millions across the world in different ways. In America, there was a near **universal fear of the spread of Communism, a willingness to serve in the military, and to pay increased taxes to support massive defense spending.** I was born in 1950 and looking back, my early memories of the Cold War were being **taught to "duck and cover"** in elementary school and visiting my friend who didn't have a father because he had been a paratrooper killed in a place called **Korea.**

I emphasize that the Cold War affected not just those serving in the military and defense industries, but also had serious effects on families and communities. Women bore the brunt of single-handedly running families during continuous long deployments, Temporary Duties (TDYs), moving every few years, and often being stationed on remote bases and children growing up in these conditions had to develop resilience early on.

In the 1950s, a student athlete from our small town went far away out west in Colorado to the fairly new **Air Force Academy** and everyone was very proud of him. I also remember going through the frequencies on a shortwave radio and finding **"Radio Moscow,"** talking with young men who had come back from far away strange-sounding places—one had been in the Air Force and had learned to write backwards on a Plexiglas status board, and hearing about some **families building fallout shelters**.

In October 1962, I had just turned 12 years old and we realized that something very bad was going on when **worried adults intensely watched TV as President Kennedy spoke** to the nation about something called *the Cuban Missile Crisis.* President Kennedy had committed the main strength of the Atlantic fleet into blockade operations to prevent Soviet ships bearing nuclear-capable rockets guarded by nuclear-capable submarines from reaching Cuba.

P-2 *Neptune* (crew 10, range 1900 NM at 180 kts) rigging Soviet freighter enroute to Cuba *US Navy Dictionary of American Naval Aviation Squadrons Volume 2: The History of VP, VPB, VP(H) and VP(AM) Squadrons*

*500 miles south of us at Naval Air Station (NAS) Norfolk, Ltjg Roger Stambaugh, a P-2 Patrol Plane Commander (PPC) had gotten a surprise:

*"On October 23rd 1962, I was at NAS Norfolk with my P-2 crew (TAD-Temporary Additional Duty from VP-19 at Alameda. California) for weapons evaluation at NAS PAX River. That evening we were in the "O" (Officers) Club when President Kennedy announced his embargo of Cuba. This was the beginning of **the Cuban Missile Crisis**. The next morning we gathered at the flight line to fly back to Alameda. ---**Surprise! My P-2 was loaded with weapons including a NUC(lear) depth charge!**

CINCLANT was just across the road so, **in flight gear, I went over to find out what the H... was going on.** Admiral Koch, commander of aviation for CINCLANT met with me and **said I now belonged to him** and we were to fly a night patrol. **The NUC? He told me to contact ops before I dropped it, if I could not make contact, use my judgement. Jeez.**

*During the patrol that evening **we found a large group of ships heading South. We had not been briefed that any of our ships were in that area so I went down and lit them up.** Much to our dismay they were ours. **We were fortunate not to be fired upon. So much for complete intel(ligence.)***

*...Think about it. **I'm a 25 year-old P-2 PPC (with 3 years in the Navy) flying off a strange beach carrying a Nuc. and lighting up our war ships. The Cold War could have heated up that night...***

At the end of WWII, 12 million Americans had been in uniform (3.4 million in the Navy alone)[10] and the national priority was to demobilize service members as quickly as possible, so the military shrank rapidly to less than 2 million by 1949. By comparison, in 1977 during my VP-45 tour, **over 2 million Americans** were on active duty with about **530,000 in the Navy** (in 2016: 1.3 million and **326,000 Navy**). In the 1950s and 60s, every man had a **Draft Number and had to go into "the Service"** at age 18 (or after four years of college) to enable the US to maintain sufficient forces around the world to contain Communist expansion.

*Retired Air Force Lieutenant Colonel Hal Donahue enlisted in the Air Force in 1966 and became an officer in 1973; he remembers his Weapons Systems Operator (WSO) flying days and the effects of the Cold War:

"WSOs got tossed into the pilot pile and in my day, we were supposed to fly at least ten minutes an hour. Except for promotions, it did not matter to most of us.

*Korea and the Vietnam War are well documented Cold War events. **Unsung and less noted are the quiet service of the military and their families abroad.** With the death of my father who was in his seventies, my wife, children and I returned home to attend the funeral. More than my father's death, what I remember most was my then ten-year-old son saying; "Dad, this is the **first funeral of an old person that we ever attended.** The others (5 deaths) were all much younger."*

---

[10] www.nationalww2museum.org

It was true. **Flying fighter aircraft was dangerous to the point that most civilian life insurance companies would only refund your premiums with interest if you died as aircrew within the first ten years.** *Not just military aircraft were lost confronting the Soviet Union and other threats around the globe--the Military and their families were* **constantly exposed to terrorist threats in every corner of the globe.** *(Germany: Red Army Faction-BaderMeinhoff Gang; Italy: 1978 Red Brigade killed former Italian Prime Minister Moro & 1981 kidnapped US Army General Dozier)*

The steady, slow loss of life was ever present from single often unnoticed attacks to the horrific terrorist attacks October 23, 1983 on US and French military forces in Beirut, Lebanon. According to CNN: **"This was the deadliest attack against US Marines since the battle over Iwo Jima in February 1945."** *Dead were 220 Marines and 21 other US military. In a separate, coordinated attack, 58 French paratroopers lost their lives to another suicide bomber.*

The Cold War was the single greatest military victory in modern history. *That it is not celebrated as such is a tribute to its success. The world expected all-out nuclear war. It is a tribute to the leaders and military on both sides that it did not happen.* **The unheralded death and sacrifice of military and their families should not be forgotten.**

***Hal Donahue Lt. Col. USAF (Ret.) enlisted in the Air Force in 1966, trained as an aircraft mechanic, graduated from Colgate University, and went through officer training in 1973. He served as a Weapons Systems Officer in F-4s and British Royal Air Force (RAF) as aircrew on *Buccaneer* and *Tornado aircraft.* He retired in 1990 and became a vice president in several foreign and domestic energy companies. Hal is a long-term advocate for veterans' affairs and has sat on non-profit boards dedicated to giving voice to veterans' interests. Hal is a freelance writer whose work has appeared in numerous publications and online.

The "Draft" was vital to maintain the millions of servicemen necessary for national defense in the Cold War. Conscription is the forced enlistment or "drafting" of young men to serve-usually in the Army. The US used conscription in the Civil War, World War I and World War II. Different regions of the country Drafted young men according to the needs of the Army. Some men knew they would be called soon so elected to "volunteer to be drafted" into the Army or tried to enlist in another Service.

To meet the growing need for an expanded military to counter and contain Communist expansion, President Truman asked Congress in March 1948 "to provide for a strengthening of National Defense through universal military training and the restoration of Selective Service."[11] This reinstituted the **WWII (16 million Americans served)** requirement for all males to register for *the Draft* with the Selective Service System for mandatory military service between ages 19-26, thereby enabling the Department of Defense to have a long-term highly qualified and geographically diverse supply of troops to man the Military Services. Throughout the Cold War, *the Draft* always loomed in young men's lives and mandatory initial Reserve Officer Training Corps (ROTC) training was required at many colleges.

1954 VP-45 P5M-1 Marlin (later P-5A and SP-5B; Crew 11, range 1800 NM at cruise speed 130 kts) *US Navy*

---

[11] Harry S. Truman, *Years of Trial and Hope-Memoirs*, Volume II, Time, Inc. Doubleday & Company, New York 1956, p. 279

*At a Patrol Squadron 45 reunion, a retired patrol senior leader *recounted that after he graduated from college* **in the late Fifties, he wanted to serve the country like his relatives and neighbors had done in WWII,** *so he went down to the Navy recruiter and asked what the shortest officer commitment was. They told him Aviation Observer (navigator) so he signed up, went to Aviation Officer Candidate School, became a patrol boat pilot, and ended up serving for over 30 years in very senior command positions. This patriotic "wanting to serve the country" mindset was an extremely important factor in providing the best candidates for military service at a time when the country needed more of them as the Cold War intensified.*

During the Korean "Police Action" **1.5 million--** and in the Vietnam "Conflict" over **1.8 million** American men were drafted.[12] The new **Volunteer Military** which began in 1973 greatly altered the traditional concept of everyone having a commitment for national military service.

*Retired Army General and former CIA Director David Petraeus (West Point 1974) put it this way:

*"In World War II, **11.2%** of the nation served in four years. During the Vietnam era, **4.3%** served in twelve years. Since 2001, only **0.45%** of our population have served in the Global War on Terror. These are unbelievable statistics. **Over time, fewer and fewer people have shouldered more and more of the burden and it is only getting worse. Our troops were sent to war in Iraq by a Congress consisting of 10% veterans with only one person having a child in the military...** "[13]*

Navy Cold War Anti-Submarine Patrols

*1950s P-2V patrol aircrewman Ron Wheeler of Albany, New York remembers Navy patrols:

*"We served at **a time when Russia, China and North Korea were at "war" with us** in a sometimes-deadly manner...patrol aircraft shot down; but more often with antagonistic, in-your-face exercises...close encounters with their aircraft...*

---

[12] Selective Service System, www.sss.gov/About/History-And-Records/ Induction-Statistics

[13] General David Petraeus, *Letter to My Fellow Veterans*, August 2012

Soviet submariners: *we respected them*

My thoughts on this Memorial Day (2007) go back 50 years, *to when I was a young crewman on a Navy P2V-7, a Lockheed Neptune patrol plane, deployed for five months to the Royal Naval Air Station in Halfar, Malta, in the Mediterranean. Our squadron designation was Patrol Squadron Twenty-Three (VP-23) and our home base was the Naval Air Station in Brunswick, Maine.*

On July 21, 1957, our squadron lost an aircraft that was on a search mission in northwestern Italy. *It was looking for a Lockheed Neptune, P2V-6, assigned to Navy Reserve Patrol Squadron,* ***VP-934, that had been reported missing....***

On July 23, 1957, within days after these two crashes, a Navy P2V-5F crashed 300 yards off Barbers Point, Hawaii, killing all 10 crew members. Fifty years ago, within a span of a less than one week, 30 Navy air crewmen died in horrific crashes not related to combat. *These young men, in the service of their country were as dead as if they had been cut down by a Japanese machine gun, a German artillery round, or an IED in Iraq. Their families' grief was, and may still be, as strong as if the loss of these men was in combat.*

There were no counselors for us in those days, no large turn-outs, no stone walls listing names to be touched, no long

lines of uniformed personnel participating in annual re-membrances, no speeches; just a simple memorial service carried out in within a few weeks after the accident. We climbed into our aircraft and continued our patrols record-ing Russian naval activity, gathering electronic intelligence, and performing search and rescue missions.

Although I'm considered a Korean War veteran, I never call myself that out of respect for those who slogged through combat in Korea. **We were the Cold War veterans, the Cold War casualties, and although we may be lost in the mix of all of the other conflicts and wars, we continued on with what our country expected from us, dedication to duty.**

These losses are but a few that took place during the Cold War. I didn't record the number of Navy aircraft and crewmen who were shot down by Russian and Chinese aircraft and Chinese shore ar-tillery. Nor did I cite the **loss of members of a Coast Guard air crew during an attempt to rescue some of these naval avia-tors -- all during the Cold War.**

So, my mind drifts back 50 years to remember those who died in carrying out their duty. Perhaps this Memorial Day, their families can obtain some satisfaction -- not closure, because I don't believe there is any such thing -- **knowing that their sons, husbands and fathers died honorably serving their country in a forgotten period of world tension.**"[14]

*** Ron Wheeler joined the Navy in 1954 and upon discharge was designated a Korean War veteran, however, he describes himself as a Korean War Era veteran and a Cold War veteran. Ron says that "The Navy gave me an opportunity to grow-up, the Korean GI Bill assisted me in getting my BA degree from Siena College, and the Navy discipline helped me through my master's Degree in Public Administration. My love for flying saw me through my Flight Instructors Certificate, (CFI, Instrument, multi) and getting the Air

---

[14] Ron Wheeler, http://www.vpnavy.com/vp23_mishap.html from the Albany Times-Union, May 29, 2007 http://www.timesunion.com/AspStories/story.asp? storyID=592743&category=OPINION&newsdate=5/28/2007

Transport Pilot's certificate. As an avocation, I wrote for various aviation publications, but mostly for *IFR Magazine*. I had to earn my living by working for the New York State Division of Criminal Justice Services. Once again, the Navy discipline and understanding of the chain of command assisted me. After retirement, I became a chief pilot for a small Part 135 operation. No bragging here, just pointing out what the military did for me, how service during a *"quiet" war* helped me. I'm glad I served and would do it over again without hesitation."

Allies in Anti-Submarine Warfare ASW has always been a cooperative Allied effort and many countries contributed significant forces to the continuous Cold War efforts to hunt and track Soviet submarines, especially when they became capable of delivering nuclear warheads in the early 1960s. Norwegian, Dutch, British, and Canadian crews were heavily involved in integrated operations including deployments to Iceland, Azores, and Sicily. French and German crews were also involved in coastal ASW efforts.

Canada has always been our closest ally and meshed their ASW operations with the United States. During the 1960s there was major push by the United States and Allies to upgrade their ASW capabilities to meet the challenge of rapidly growing Soviet submarine forces.

1955 Bermuda Norm Donovan (back row, second from right)
RCAF *Lancaster* (crew: 2 Pilots, 2 Navs, 3 Radio Officers and 1

FE) carried sonobuoys, torpedoes, depth charges, radar & ECM; guns in nose and rear turret. Range 2200 nm at 200 MPH

*Major Norm Donovan served in the Royal Canadian Air Force (RCAF) from 1953-1990 and was selected for exchange duty with American VP forces hunting Soviet submarines in the 1960s:

*"I joined the RCAF in 1953, wings and commission in July 1954, posted to Maritime Command on the East Coast (ZX (Greenwood), SU (Summerside), HX (Halifax). I was the RCAF Exchange Officer at Pax (Patuxent River, Maryland) from Nov '67 to Jul '70. **I was the first RCAF Navigator to be assigned to USN Patrol Squadrons which were designated as "Task Group Delta" squadrons.***

I was selected from Maritime Patrol and Evaluation Unit (MP&EU), previous tours with 405 MP Sqn, our MP Rag 2MOTU, the Joint Maritime Warfare School in Halifax then MP&EU. I joined VP44 in Nov 67 qualified as a P-3A/B TACCO. Then when TG (Task Group) Delta duties were handed over to VP24 I joined them in Aug 68 until Jul 70 as a P-3B TACCO and the squadron TG Delta Officer. (according to VPNavy.com/vp24 "Throughout the early 1960's the "BATMEN" were attached to Task Group Delta where they helped develop and accelerate the implementation of air ASW tactics and doctrine in order to improve the readiness of the Atlantic Fleet.")

*A very significant evolution occurred in **1969** when a **Yankee SLBM was tracked from his home port to his patrol station in the southern North Atlantic. VP-24, deployed at Kef and Lajes, was assigned this task. I flew 15 sorties** during this tracking evolution, of which **11** were conducted in a 20-day period. Minimum crew rest resulted in very hard and exhausting flying."*

(Note: Flying 11 8-10 hour patrols in 20 days is absolutely amazing and a tribute to these crews).

Canadian and other Allies suffered casualties during Cold war flying as evidenced by this report: "404 Squadron was deployed to Puerto Rico on an Exercise. On the night of **23 March 1965, Argus 20727 plunged into the ocean 60 miles north of the island. All**

15 perished, including two government research scientists." [15]

*Fast-forward to later years in the Cold War; between 1976-1986, seven P-3s were lost and over 70 died during peacetime operations. By the 1980s, the Cold War had been underway for **over 35 years** and tensions had escalated between the Superpowers, especially in Europe with US placement of Intermediate Range *Pershing* missiles. Jacob Heilbrunn notes that "At the core of the Cold War was the division of Germany. All Soviet attempts to extrude the United States from West Berlin after 1945 had failed. Chancellor Helmut Kohl was a staunch *Atlanticist* **who resisted a ferocious Soviet campaign to block the installation of intermediate-range Pershing missiles in 1983.**"[16]

The US and USSR had rapidly built-up their submarine, surface, and aviation capabilities and confronted each other around the world. The Reagan Administration worked to build-up the *600 ship Navy*. Between 1982-87, **President Reagan and Navy Secretary Lehman** sent carrier battle groups and submarines into the Sea of Japan, the Sea of Okhotsk, and the Norwegian Sea and NATO held *Ocean Safari* exercises in 1984 and 1987 involving hundreds of ships operating far north into the Norwegian Sea.

In the mid-1980s, I was a Patrol Plane Commander (PPC) in VP-49 at JAX where we practiced new tactics for combined ops for *Over the Horizon Targeting* with F/A-18s from NAS Cecil Field in *War at Sea* exercises; we found ship targets and used data link to communicate with the F/A-18s. Our squadron also helped test how the P-3C handled with *Harpoon* anti-ship missiles hung under the wings.

During these years of Superpower confrontations, William M. Arkin wrote in *The Washington Post* in late 1984 that: "...the United States conducted its largest peacetime fleet exercise since World War II...**five aircraft-carrier battle groups, two of which closed within 50 miles of the Soviet city of Vladivostok.** The Soviets responded with over 100 fighter, bomber and reconnaissance overflights and put surface ships on alert." [17]

---

[15] http://www.rcaf-arc.forces.gc.ca/en/14-wing/history.page

[16] Jacob Heilbrunn, *The Prudent Pragmatist, The New York Times Book Review*, December 10, 2017, p.30

[17] William M. Arkin, *Our Risky Naval Strategy Could Get Us All Killed*, *The Washington Post*, July 3, 1988

1985 VP-49 Crew 7 Stanton/Klapka flight-test *Harpoon* shapes

An Anti-Submarine Warfare (ASW) Night Attack from 20,000 ft down to 300 ft

By the mid-1980s according to New York Times reporters, Sherry Sontag and Christopher Drew, "The Soviets were being more aggressive than ever in the Atlantic. They had just **sent a cluster of five Victor-class attack subs and for three weeks kept them so close to the East Coast of the United State that tracking them almost used up the Atlantic Fleets store of sonobuoys.**"[18]

*Our TACCO Ted Klapka (Tactical Coordinator of patrol plane's navigation, acoustic and non-acoustic sensors) recalls how ASW tensions had ratcheted-up in the mid-1980s and affected the new orders we received:

*"In the mid-1980s, tensions peaked between the US and USSR-when in response to US Pershing and Cruise missiles being placed in Europe, the **Soviets surged many of their submarines and violated the unwritten rules of the game by placing them (like our US missiles placed in Europe) much closer to our coasts inside of Bermuda and Hawaii. This was termed Analogous Response.***

---

[18] Sherry Sontag and Christopher Drew, *Blind Man's Bluff*, PublicAffairs New York 1998 p. 252

The Soviet Boomers close to the coast drastically reduced the time of flight to hit their US targets. **This complicated the US' ability to make a counter strike and was considered by the US to be a violation of the unwritten rules of the Cold War. It shifted the Mutually Assured Destruction calculus and caused the US to raise its nuclear response posture to a hair trigger in order to avoid a lose 'em before you can use 'em situation.**

The US wanted to get the Soviets to have their Subs fall back to their prior patrol positions. We had been flying for weeks on these "close aboard" submarines and they were extraordinarily closely monitored lest we lose track of these very dangerous and threatening boats. It was **unusual to fly missions from Jax(sonville Florida) and Brunswick (Maine) on top of Soviets, typically those missions were flown from Kef(lavik Iceland), Lajes (Azores), and Bermuda.** *But with Analogous Response, we and the (aircraft carrier-based) S-3 Vikings were maintaining close track from the CONUS (Continental US) bases and Bermuda. I think the* **same was going on with Hawaii and Moffett (California) ASW airborne forces.**

One day, flying out of home port of JAX(Jacksonville FL), we were getting ready to fly this new normal when we were given a special and detailed briefing at the ASWOC. We were to load **explosive SUS** *(Sound Underwater Signal), rather than the electronic noisemaker SUS...these were essentially hand grenades. Up to this point,* **all of our prior missions were standard VP anti-SLBM (Submarine Launched Ballistic Missile) covert track missions. We tracked them passively from high altitude so they didn't know we were there.** *This mission was going to be different.*

We were told that if we received a message with the code words Smoothtouch Active and a time, that we were to conduct low altitude simulated attacks with the explosive SUS at that time. We were to do the simulated attacks just like we would in wartime. The first attack would be passive, e.g., the sub would never know we were there until the SUS exploded alongside him. We were then cleared for active sonobuoys and MAD (Magnetic Anomaly Detection) tracking, while continuing the explosive SUS attacks.

But we were to cease all SUS, MAD and active tracking precisely at 30 minutes after the initially directed time of attack. This was an ASW Crew's "wet dream."

And it wasn't a solo act, but a group effort...if the Smoothtouch message was sent to all aircraft, all aircraft in the Atlantic would joint join in a covert coordinated SUS Attack at the same time. There were probably 6 or so aircraft simultaneously onstation just off the East Coast.

*We thought this was a very interesting briefing, and went to the ordnance magazine to get the SUS, but frankly, we figured there was zero chance of getting Smoothtouch tasking. So we figured it would be **another long night at 20000 ft covertly tracking our assigned boat.** However, as we started our mission things started to go differently.*

*We weren't relieving another flight and were supposed to pick up a slightly cold track on a Soviet Boomer between Jax and Bermuda. As we started to drop our initial search pattern, my Sensor 1 Jim Hesse called **"Contact!" "Soviet!" and "Hey TACCO, you better come back here" in quick succession.** Yes, we were onstation, hot on a Soviet Sub, but it wasn't a Boomer (submarine with nuclear missiles). Now what?!? We were supposed to remain covert and in radio silence.*

*I conferred with my PPC (Patrol Plane Commander) Don Stanton and we decided to place some buoys way in front of the sub and dash over toward Bermuda to call their ASWOC on secure UHF which had a lower chance of detection. After a few minutes of confusion, they finally understood that we had located a Soviet Sub, but it wasn't our Boomer. They cogitated a bit and I suspect they pulled some magic from behind the green door and called us back and told us to forget about the sub we had, they would send an S-3 out for that, but to **go look in a new location for "our Boomer."***

Ok, on to new tasking. It was now dark and it wasn't long until our new pattern went "Hot" with "our Boomer." We were flying AQA-7 V10/11/12 (if I recall correctly) that had the Passive Tracking Algorithm, so once we passively detected "our Boomer" we had good solid high-quality passive track. Our NavCom (Navigator Communicator) Jim McCrary was religiously copying the VP broadcast on the hope we would get a Smoothtouch message, but we figured was about as likely as a Santa Claus sighting.

Midnight came and went, and our IFT (In Flight Technician) and Orion Chief Mike Terry kept the tube humming and us happy with vittles and coffee. AND THEN IT HAPPENED! "99 (to all) VP SMOOTHTOUCH ALFA TIME XXYY (about 20 minutes in the future)"

WOW!!!! Don came aft from the flight station to look at the message. He and I were both incredulous. We had won the lottery. "FLIGHT, CREW- TACCO: SET CONDITION ONE FOR ASW Attack!"

*So, Flight (cockpit-pilots and flight engineer) **re-lit #1 engine and we dropped from 20,000 ft to 300 ft and prepared for an attack.** We did our best to remain covert while circling this Boomer, who was carrying out his mission to remain hidden and ready to end life on earth, as we placed both passive buoys and active "Cadillac" buoys around our unsuspecting quarry.*

*--Crew Seven was a seasoned crew, we had **been together almost three years** and we worked as one. Don had the airplane perfectly positioned for us to mark on top the sub on an attack heading exactly at the ordered Smoothtouch time.*

"FLIGHT! TACCO: BOMBBAY AND MASTER ARM! SENSOR 3 STANDBY MAD!. ORDIE (Ordnanceman) STANDBY SMOKE! JEZ STANDBY ACTIVE!!!! "

As we came up from behind the Sub we were at 300 ft and 190 Kts, the sub was probably at 300 ft depth and about 5 kts. I remember his course was to the Southwest. A few seconds of quiet as we thundered forward. We had our SUS bungeed to the racks in the BOMBBAY. I had fiddled with the Torpedo Presetter just as if we had real war shot torpedoes (we didn't) and I had a torp(edo) drop selected online. My finger hovered over the weapons release button. I also had buoys selected.

As we passed over the submarines track, our Sensor 3 "Campy" Pendleton sang out "MADMAN! MADMAN! MADMAN!" The sub was right where we thought it was. Nav Jim McCrary smashed the button causing the HSP teletype to rattle away just as my fingers stabbed at Weapons Release and Buoy Release sending an explosive SUS and two buoys. Clunk! The bomb rack released the SUS. Ordie cried out, "Smoke Away!"

At about this same time, "our Boomer" was jerked from quiet routine and boredom of the Midwatch (midnight to 0400) by the 17 and 68 hertz thunder of four P-3 props passing overhead. I imagined thought clouds over Ivan's heads with the Cyrillic equivalent of "WTF?!?"

*I had one of the nearby buoys dialed up and heard the explosion of the **grenade-sized SUS explode close aboard the sub.** What seemed only nanoseconds later, SS1 Hesse was banging buttons to have the **active buoys** we laid on him banging away. PING!! PING!! PING!! We had **Cadillac** (best very expensive) **buoys** all around the sub and had him "suitcased." I also suspect the boomer's laundry just got a lot more to do. Explosive SUS use was rare, and likely they thought it was a real depth charge. Active Buoys? Those were never used on Boomers. Have these Amerikanskis lost their minds?*

*The Boomer initially responded like it was "game on" but then as **he could hear the distant BANGs of the other aircraft he reacted like his life depended on it**...at this point he probably thought it did. **He yanked, he banked, he dived, he spit noisemakers and decoys. We pinged away on our active buoys.** And then I heard another Bang! The sound of an exploding SUS probably a hundred miles away as another crew did their Smoothtouch...and another and another.*

The sub had to believe World War 3 had started. We banked around for our next "simulated attack. "STANDBY MAD. STANDBY SMOKE." SUS AND BUOYS SELECTED. "MADMAN! MADMAN! MADMAN!" Clunk! As the bomb rack under us released another SUS. Bang!

I remembered the phrase "Nantucket Sleigh Ride" describing when "iron men in wooden boats" harpooned whales and careened through the sea their line tethering them to a wounded leviathan.

This seemed the same. We treated ourselves as tethered to this writhing beast full of scared men as they tried to break away. But one side played with blank pistols scaring the crap out of the other side carrying nuclear-tipped missiles.

*We got off about **5 or 6 attacks** on a submarine that was desperate to break its pursuer...he probably wondered when we would actually get the next "depth charge" on him. And he could hear other explosions coming from many directions as well as the distant pinging of our mates. He could probably hear the propellers of his mates as they thrashed to get away.*

*And then...silence. After 30 minutes, we and the other aircraft resumed passive and covert tracking. We climbed back up to altitude and quit actively poking the bear. I went aft to look at the (sonar)Grams. They were quite a sight, and still continued to be for a few moments as the **subs at emergency flank bells thrashed away**. And then, I guess they figured out we had been playing with "blanks" and slowed down to resume their routine.*

Our relief (aircraft) arrived shortly thereafter and we smugly turned over Hot contact to them.

Back to Jax and debrief. Hard not to get a 100 OSE after this event. That cold beer in the Wing parking lot never tasted so good.

A day or two later, the Soviet Subs quietly moved to their old patrol positions on the other side of Bermuda. It appears the Soviets got the message, "that could have been real, and the next time it will be."

As a young twenty-something Lieutenant during the Reagan years, that night seemed the ultimate game. Upon reflection, it all now gives me great pause..."

*** Ted Klapka graduated from University of Illinois Navy ROTC and served on USS Berkeley (DDG-15) and qualified as a Surface Warfare Officer in 1980. He was designated a Naval Flight Officer in 1983 and served in VP-49, on VP Wing staffs, and finished as the VP P-3 Chief Engineer in PMA-290. Ted works as L-3s Director of Naval Aviation Liaison at NAS Patuxent River Maryland.

Chapter 2
A Cold War Primer: the 1940s-1950s

The Cold War began in 1947 (some use 1945--the end of WWII) with the Soviet takeover of Eastern Europe and *the Truman Doctrine* to contain Communism and ended with the disintegration of the Soviet Union in 1991. The momentous events of World War II set the stage for the 44 years of the Cold War.

In 1939 Joseph Stalin and Adolf Hitler surprised the world by secretly concluding the *Nazi-Soviet Pact* which divided Europe into spheres of influence from Finland south to the Black Sea. After Germany launched its surprise attack on the Soviet Union in 1941, the US and Britain quickly reacted to assist Russia via the *Lend Lease* program (negotiated by American Special Envoy W. Averill Harriman and British Lord Beaverbrook). At the **1943 Yalta Conference** Roosevelt, Churchill, and Stalin negotiated how Europe would be reorganized after the war.

In 1945, Europe reeled in post-war chaos with millions killed or wounded, millions displaced and moving, destroyed factories and infrastructure, broken economies, and unstable governments. Greece, Italy, France, and Germany were unstable and vulnerable to growing strong Communist movements. While **Stalin had agreed to hold elections** for Eastern European countries after WWII, the **Soviet Union reneged** and brutally established Communist satellite regimes using subversion, political, military, economic, and active intelligence measures.

During 1945-46, the US and its allies were focused on demobilizing millions of citizen soldiers and quickly transitioning from a wartime to a peacetime economy; we were looking inward while the Soviets aggressively consolidated their military conquests and created buffer states in Eastern Europe. Most Americans just wanted to make up for lost time, get on with their lives, and they were not that interested in foreign problems.

President Truman observed in his memoirs that "What we have been living through is, in fact, is **a period of nationalistic, social and economic tensions.** These tensions were in part brought about by shattered nations trying to recover from the war and by peoples in many places awakening to their right to freedom. **More than half of the world's population was subject for centuries to foreign domination and economic slavery."**[19]

1947 Germany *"We Want Coal and Bread" Deutches Bundesarchive*

Soviet Takeover of Eastern Europe In June 1945, a Polish coalition provisional government, dominated by Communists, rounded-up 16 opposition leaders--including **heroes of the *Polish Home Army (which had risen up against the Nazis in August 1944 against the Nazis for 63 days),*** put them on a show trial, and executed all but a few. President Truman noted that "A Russian Red Army Marshall was sent to take over the Polish Army. At about the same time, Stalin "invited" little Finland to sign a pact of friendship" with the Soviet Union...To the people of Europe who were just starting to take courage from the Marshall Plan, **these Communist moves looked like the beginning of a Russian "big push."**[20]

---

[19] Harry S. Truman, Op. Cit., p. x
[20] Truman, Op.Cit., p. 278

In early 1946, American diplomat George Kennan sent his famous *Long Telegram* from Moscow laying out the need to contain Communism by all means including force and Winston Churchill gave his landmark *Sinews of Peace* **speech** at Westminster College in Missouri, stating that *"From Stettin in the Baltic to Trieste in the Adriatic, an **iron curtain** has descended across the Continent."* [21]

WWII had bankrupted Britain so the government embarked on a crash program to stabilize its budget in early 1947 and unilaterally announced withdrawal of its aid for Greece and Turkey. During the savage **Greek Civil War** (1946-49) the US was forced to take the Allied lead and intervene quickly to prevent strong Communist forces from taking power. Congress approved funding to oppose the potential Communist takeover in Greece and to bolster efforts in other countries.

During 1947 **Hungarian Communists** seized power while the Premier was traveling, the **Bulgarian** opposition leader was hung, the **Romanian king** was forced to abdicate and a key opposition leader was sentenced to lifetime solitary confinement. In early 1948, a Soviet-backed coup succeeded in the last Eastern European multi-party state, **Czechoslovakia**, and foreign minister Jan Masaryk mysteriously fell to his death from a window. There was also a great danger that Italy would fall to communism and the US exerted efforts to support the Christian Democrat victory in the 1948 election.

In 1947 President Truman, Secretary of State Marshall, and Under Secretary Acheson embarked on the **Truman Doctrine** to contain Communist expansion throughout the world via coordinated diplomatic, economic *(Marshall Plan)*, and military means. Secretary Marshall stated that "Our policy is directed not against any country or doctrine, but **against hunger, poverty, desperation and chaos. Its purpose should be the revival of a working economy in the world so as to permit the emergence of political and social conditions in which free institutions can exist."** [22]

---

[21] Winston Churchill, Sinews of Peace speech, March 5, 1946 at Westminster College, www.nationalchurchillmuseum.org/sinews-of-peace-iron-curtain-speech.html

[22] Secretary of State George C. Marshall, speech to the Harvard Alumni Association, June 5, 1947

Between 1948-1952, the *Marshall Plan* **provided about $120B** in today's dollars to help European countries recover from WWII, to develop economically, and to counter Communist advances. In 1947, 48 states contributed 700 railcars (known as *the Friendship Train)* of food, fuel, and clothing worth $40 million to assist France and Italy recover from the war. In 1949, France sent *the Merci Train* filled with gifts to thank the American states.

C-47s (crew 4, range 1600 nm at 140 kts) in
1948 unloading at Tempelhof Berlin *USAF*

The Berlin Blockade and the Berlin Airlift On June 18, 1948, the western Allies, Britain, France, and the United States, instituted currency reforms and initiated the new Deutsche Mark in their zones which infuriated the Soviets (over-printed stamp above). General Secretary Stalin ordered the blockade all truck, rail, and water supply routes to Berlin to force the Allied Powers (Britain, France, and the US) out of the city.

President Truman reacted quickly on June 29, 1948 affirming, ***"We stay in Berlin, period."*** and ordered the organization of an immediate massive Allied airlift to fly fuel and food to resupply the city of over 2 million. He also ***"sent two squadrons of B-29s to Germany, the giant planes known to the world as the kind that dropped the atomic bombs on Japan. But in fact, these had not*** *been modified to carry atomic bombs, a detail the Russians did not know."*[23]

On extremely short notice, American crews were ordered to Germany from Air Force bases all over the world including Alaska, Hawaii, and Guam. Former aircrew received telegrams to report immediately for rushed training to augment cargo aircraft.

Around midnight on a Saturday, the **crews of C-54s based halfway around the world in Guam** were suddenly notified of their movement to Germany by their Group Commander:

"Gentlemen! Your group is asked to leave for Hawaii immediately, from there to California, Massachusetts and Wiesbaden, Germany, from where you will participate in the airlift to West Berlin. Take your ground personnel, your radio operators, your technical personnel....Confirm receipt of this message...**We fly in two hours, gentlemen**...(Some asked:) What about our families?...(the Answer:) The Air Force will take care of them."*

As C-54s ordered from Mobile Alabama via Westover AFB in Massachusetts arrived in Newfoundland for their Atlantic crossing via the Azores to Germany they were told, "Press on as you can, ignore minor maintenance." An hour and fifteen minutes after arriving at [24] *Rhein-Main Air Base in Germany, one of the Alabama C-54s was headed for West Berlin."*

The Soviets finally backed down and President Truman's resolute commitment to supply Berlin had been a key turning point in the emerging Cold War. "The airlift was over, after a year and two months, **277,804** flights, and the delivery of **2,325,809 tons** of food and supplies."[25]

Richard Reeves writes that, "Uncelebrated airmen, mechanics, weathermen, ground controllers, and uncommon laborers who were among the **60,000** men and women who kept the airlift going for more than a year...What was it like to be one of the **17,000**

[23] David McCullough, *Truman,* New York, Simon & Schuster, 1992, pp. 630- 631

[24] Richard Reeves, *Daring Young Men-The Heroism and Triumph of the Berlin Airlift June 1948-May 1949,* New York, Simon & Schuster, 2010 pp. 40-43

[25] McCullough, op. cit. 734

German women and men, wearing whatever clothes they had, sometimes slippers and bathing suits, using the rubble of their broken and cruelly hungry city to build a new airfield at Tegel in just **92 days**?"...*The Berlin Airlift **"...cost the lives of 73 Allied airmen...39 British citizens, RAF regulars and civilians, and 32 Americans were killed during the airlift, along with 9 or more German airlift employees."**[26]

Convair B-36 *Peacemaker* (Crew 13; **100** gallons oil & **56 spark plugs** per engine) *USAF*

The Primacy of Strategic Bombers Responding to voters' demands to cut wartime spending, President Truman radically slashed the defense budget after the war ended. His Secretary of Defense, Louis Johnson decreed that: conventional weapons spending would be cut and the new Air Force's strategic bombers would be the nation's nuclear delivery platform; that Marine Corps Aviation would be folded into the Air Force, the Navy's newest carrier class *USS United States* was cancelled, and the Navy's budget downsized.

The Administration heavily favored the new Air Force and planned funding for 1,000 strategic bombers at the expense of the other Services' conventional forces. These dramatic changes led to Congressional hearings in 1949 and the **Admirals' Revolt** (many were fired) against the radical budget cuts. The Navy survived

---

[26] Reeves, op. cit., pp. xv-xvii, 271

and eventually funding was provided for the new *Forrestal* class super-carrier which could handle a heavier nuclear-capable bomber.

Early Navy Strategic Delivery Efforts

An EA-3B (Crew 7, range 1800nm at 450 kts) variant
of the original A-3 *(the Whale) US Navy*

Until the mid-1960s when the **Polaris** submarine-launched ballistic missile (SLBM) became operational, the Navy's contributions to the **nuclear Triad** were the Douglas A-3 *Skywarrior* attack bomber and the *Regulus* nuclear missile. The Navy even experimented with launching land-based patrol P-2V aircraft from aircraft carriers. The A-3 was designed to give the Navy a **10,000 lb. atomic bomb delivery capability** to compete with the Air Force's new B-36 and B-47 strategic bombers. The Navy also developed the nuclear-capable **Regulus surface-to-surface missile** capable of 500-1000 NM range, eventually fitted with an early Inertial Navigation System (INS). *Regulus* was deployed on aircraft carriers and cruisers (strategic patrols 1955-1961) and submarines (strategic patrols from 1959-64) to provide the Navy with a nuclear capability before the **Polaris**-equipped submarines became operational.

Regulus II missile on *USS Grayback (SSG-584; crew 84, 12 kts submerged) US Navy*

The Soviets surprised the world with their successful **1949 atomic bomb test** (aided by extensive espionage by Theodore Hall, Saville Sax,[27] Klaus Fuchs,[28] Harry Gold, David Greenglass, the Rosenbergs, and others) which shocked the US into accelerating efforts to maintain nuclear superiority. The Soviets atomic success plunged the US and its Allies into the costly arms race of nuclear deterrence and decades of military build-ups.

Communist "Red" China In 1949, **Mao Zedong** and the People's Liberation Army (PLA) finally pushed Chiang Kai-shek's Nationalists out of China to the island of Formosa (now Taiwan). The Nationalists stationed tens of thousands of troops on the islands of **Quemoy (Kinmen) and Matsu** near China to maintain military pressure on the Communists. In 1950 President Truman declared the Straits of Formosa to be neutral and ordered the Seventh Fleet to patrol the Straits.

In 1954-55 the PLA maintained massive artillery bombardments of the islands and in 1955, senior US officials talked openly of using tactical nuclear weapons to defend Taiwan's interests there. In 1958 China increased bombardment of the islands and the nationalists responded with hundreds killed on both sides, including air battles;

---

[27] Alan S. Cowell, *"Theodore Hall, Prodigy and Atomic Spy, Dies at 74"*. *New York Times*, November 10, 1999

[28] Schwartz, Michael I., *"The Russian-A Bomb: The Role of Espionage in the Soviet Atomic Bomb Project"* Harvard University Press, 1996

eventually it devolved to shelling with propaganda leaflets. Navy patrol planes flew missions during these tense times and were sometimes intercepted and shot-down by Chinese jets.

During **the Korean War** (1950-53) 1.5 million men were drafted and over 33,000 Americans were killed.[29] *The initial US line to contain Communist expansion ran from Japan via Taiwan, Philippines, Malaya, and Indonesia.* However, when the **North Korean Peoples' Army (KPA)** with Chinese and Soviet support attacked the South in June 1950, the US had few forces to bolster the South Koreans. The US was initially unprepared to meet the rapid KPA attacks since it had been concentrating resources and efforts in building up the strategic nuclear bomber force, at the expense of conventional forces.

Due to President Truman's massive budget cuts to conventional forces, the US was unprepared and had to scrape together forces (such as taking tanks from museums and displays to get enough for operations) to respond. The US initially sent lightly-armed reinforcements from Japan (***Task Force Smith***, 1/3 of whose members were killed). The South Koreans and Americans were steadily driven back to the **Pusan Perimeter** in the southeast.

In September 1950, General MacArthur mounted an amphibious invasion of **Inchon** which led to the liberation of the capital, Seoul, and movement above the 38th parallel. 21 nations participated in the **United Nations' defense of South Korea**. In October 1950, Chinese Peoples' Volunteer Army troops secretly marched at night into Korea and drove UN forces back. The USSR sent pilots, aircraft, and supplies to support communist efforts. The war in Korea developed into several years of grinding losses, finally ending with an armistice in June 1953. After UN sanctions were set on North Korea because of its ICBM build-up, Kim Jong-un declared in 2013 that the armistice was over and a state of war continues to exist.

The North Atlantic Treaty Organization (NATO) was formed in 1949 to provide mutual defense and act as a united bulwark against Communism. NATO initially included the US, Canada, United Kingdom, France, Belgium, Netherlands, Luxembourg, Italy,

---

[29] Selective Service System, May 27, 2003. *Induction Statistics. In Inductions (by year) from World War I Through the End of the Draft (1973) Archived* May 7, 2009

Portugal, Norway, Denmark, and Iceland. While the US stood against the reestablishment of colonial empires after WWII, **the French made their participation in NATO conditional on returning to their colonial interests in Indochina.**

President Truman observed that "The Marshall Plan had brought some relief, but the constant threat of unpredictable Soviet moves resulted in an atmosphere of insecurity and fear among the peoples of Western Europe. Something more needed to be done to counteract the fear of the peoples of Europe that their countries would be overrun by the Soviet Army before effective help could arrive. **Only an inclusive security system (NATO) could dispel these fears...We hoped it (the NATO treaty) would serve to prevent World War III."**[30]

During the 1950s, 60s & 70s the US and its allies worked to *contain Communism*, fought wars in **Korea** (over 58,000 South Korean, 36,000 American, 1000 British, 500 Canadian, and many thousands of Allies' deaths) **Vietnam** (over 254,000 South Vietnamese, 58,000 American, 5000 South Korean, 400 Australian, and other Allies' deaths) and supported many **proxy confrontations** with the communist world. We deployed resources, intelligence support, and sometimes forces to counter Soviet support for communist *National Liberation Fronts* (NLFs) in the *Third World* (the term used then; now known as *Developing countries*).

---

[30] Harry S. Truman, op. cit., pp. 286, 288

Chapter 3
In Harm's Way: Cold War Casualties

1955 VP-9 MiG-15 attack survivors *US Navy*
via *www.vpnavy.org/vp9_mishaps*

Navy Patrol & Reconnaissance Losses

While Americans at home were settling in and enjoying post-WWII prosperity, our defense was being guaranteed by millions of young men and women who were serving on US bases, remote outposts, and manning ships and planes around the world.

In the early years of the Cold War—*well before the development of reconnaissance satellites*--the US desperately needed timely **intelligence, photographs, and air samples** (to determine atomic weapons progress) on Soviet capabilities. We were groping to gain information about Soviet capabilities in any way and Air Force and Navy reconnaissance and patrol aircraft were often sent into *Harm's Way,* hem-stitching and sometimes penetrating the Soviet, Red Chinese, and North Korean coasts in international airspace, on patrols and intelligence-gathering missions.

Several friends died on *peacetime* military flying operations and while I had some sense of sacrifices made during the Cold War, I was shocked to learn the magnitude of these losses. According to *VP International's* Book of Remembrance: ***"Since 1947, there have been 1149 American casualties" on Navy patrol missions; some patrol crews were shot down by Soviet, Chinese or North Korean fighters:***

- "April 1950 VP-26 PB-4 Shot down by Russian fighter while patrolling international waters of the Baltic Sea 10 killed
- November 1951 VP-6 P-2V Shot down by Russian fighter aircraft over international waters off the Sea of Japan 10 killed
- July 1952 VP-731 PBM-5 Attacked by Chinese fighters, off West Korea 2 killed
- January 1953 VP-22 P-2V Badly damaged by Anti-Aircraft fire from Swatow Island (Red China) that it was forced to ditch 2 killed *"(**11 of 13** crewmen were rescued by a US **Coast Guard PBM-5 Mariner, under fire from Chinese shore batteries** on Nan Ao Tao island. **Attempting to takeoff in 8-12 foot swells, the PBM crashed. 10 survivors out of 19** total (including **5** from the P2V-5) were rescued by the destroyer USS Halsey Powell (DD-686)."*[31]
- September 1954 VP-19 P-2V Shot down by Russian fighter **40 nms.** off Siberia; Ditched, the crew survived except for the Navigator 1 killed
- June 1955, a Navy VP-9 P-2V was attacked by Soviet MiG-15s over the Bering Sea and managed to crash-land on St. Laurence Island, Alaska; the crew survived.
- August 1956 a Chinese fighter shot down a Navy *VQ-1* P-4M at night 32 miles off the coast of Wenchow, China and **all 16** crewmen were killed
- April 1969 N. Korean MiG-17s shot down *VQ-1* EC-121M **90 nms.** off Korea; 31 crewmen killed" *greatest single aircraft loss in the Cold War*
- **20** Navy WV/EC121 radar picket aircraft accidents with

---

[31] *http://sw.propwashgang.org/shootdown_list.html*

113 deaths[32]

- December 1977 VP-11 crashed into mountains Canary Islands **13** killed
- April 1978 VP-23 water impact off Azores **7** killed
- September 1978 VP-8 wing separation in flight Maine **7** killed
- October 1978 VP-9 Engine overspeed and fire, subsequent ditching Adak Alaska **5** killed
- June 1979 VP-22 Engine failure with subsequent fire Cubi Point Philippines **5** killed
- April 1980 VP-50 A/C struck tram wires Pago Pago **6** killed
- June 1983 VP-1 crashed into mountain Hawaii **14** killed
- March 1990 VP-50 lost **2 P-3Cs, 27 dead.** Midair collision during a turnover procedure in the Pacific. *This could be considered the last USN mishap during the Cold War"* [33]

A word about our VQ cousins who over the decades have quietly done amazing work for national security. In 1955, *Fleet Air Reconnaissance* squadrons VAQ-1 and VAQ-2 were stood-up to provide electronic countermeasures and signals intelligence. Both squadrons initially flew P-4M *Mercators*, then EC-121s, EP-3Es, and EA-3Bs. VQ helped VP in many important ways and were often watching and guarding us when we flew into tight spots. We saw their crews when we were on detachments to the NATO base at Souda Bay, Crete. The EA-3Bs (called *Whales* because they were the largest carrier aircraft and took up so much deck space) were electronic intelligence variants of the Douglas A-3 *Skywarriors* which had been the Navy's nuclear delivery platform until the mid-60s.

Air Force Radar Picket and Reconnaissance Losses

- 11 radar EC-121s in accidents killing **66** aircrew and 3 were lost over the Atlantic resulting in **50** deaths

---

[32] Boys, Dean "Connie losses (total)" *www.dean-boys.com* May 22, 2007
[33] *VP International "Book of Remembrance" Norm Donovan* http://vpinternational.ca/

- In Vietnam 2 USAF *"Batcat"* aircraft were lost in accidents killing **22** aircrew[34]

Air Force crews often flew secretly into the Soviet Union, Eastern Europe, and Red China to collect intelligence. Many crews did not come back and it is still hard to gain information on these missions, but it appears that some died in captivity. William E. Burrows wrote an excellent book about secret Air Force Intelligence flights and official cover-ups of casualties; he notes that **163 aircrewmen and 16 aircraft were lost during the Cold War**.[35]

Some Air Force reconnaissance casualties:

- January 1953, Soviet fighters shot down a B-29 which was dropping leaflets in Manchuria. **11 of the 14-man crew parachuted out and survived but were imprisoned in China and not released until 1956**.
- July 1953 Soviet MiGs shot down an RB-50 over international waters **90 miles off Vladivostok**
- 1955, Soviet MiG-15s shot down an RB-47 near the Kamchatka peninsula and the crew were **all killed**
- July 1960, An ERB-47 was shot down in the Barents Sea north of the Kola Peninsula; 4 of the **6 crewmen perished and 2 were held by the Soviets for many months**. [36]
- May 1960 Soviet SAMs shot down Captain Power's U-2C
- October 1962 SAMs shot down and killed Major Anderson in his U-2F during Cuban Missile Crisis
- 1965 North Korean MiG 17s intercepted ERB-47H and *knocked out 3 engines; it still managed to land Yokota AB Japan*
- September 1983, as USAF RC-135s monitored an upcoming Soviet missile test, a Soviet fighter shot down a Boeing 747, Korean Air Lines Flight 007, which had strayed off its airway and flown over the Kamchatka peninsula; 269 passengers/crew perished.

---

[34] Boys, Dean, Op. Cit., May 22 2007

[35] William E. Burrows, *By Any Means Necessary: America's Secret Air War in the Cold War.* New York: Farrar, Straus and Giroux, 2001

[36] *Propwashgang, op. cit.*

Chapter 4
At Home During the Cold War

1950 US National Security Resources Board Civil Defense Office

Nuclear Weapons The United States moved quickly to accelerate the development and testing of atomic weapons and fielding strategic and tactical units to utilize them. **President Truman stated that "By the end of 1952 twenty separate nuclear detonations** had been set off at the Nevada testing grounds on Yucca Flats, and a great number of different devices had been tested. Troops had been brought in to test defensive equipment and tactics, and several battalions of the Army were already equipped with new-type cannon capable **of firing atomic shells."**[37]

In the 1950s, The US (and the Soviets) worked to develop a much more powerful *"Hydrogen"* **(thermonuclear fusion) bomb** and tested it in November 1952 on Eniwetok atoll in the Pacific,

---

[37] Harry S. Truman, op. cit., p. 357

followed closely by a successful Soviet test in August 1953. The extreme power and intensity of the hydrogen bomb was reported; "As the heat grew in intensity, observers thirty miles away began to get concerned. The wings of a B-36 flying at 40,000 feet fifteen miles from the explosion **heated 93 degrees within seconds**.... the giant cloud mushrooming up from the explosion had reached the stratosphere, and it then spread out in a huge canopy that eventually was more than one hundred miles in diameter."[38]

These far more powerful bombs escalated the nuclear arms race, increased the potential dangers to civilians, and created public protests around the world against atmospheric testing. These tests spread radioactive particles far from the actual test sites via high-altitude wind currents which mobilized far-flung populations to oppose nuclear bomb testing.

In his final address, President Truman optimistically observed that "We have averted World War III up to now, and we may have already succeeded in establishing conditons which can keep that war from happening as far ahead as man can see."[39]

During the 1950s the US embarked on accelerated nuclear bomb-building programs, *eventually* **constructing about one bomb a day** to build up the nuclear arsenal. The Air Force and Navy had the *B-57* in their inventories from 1963-93; the Navy had an ASW "special weapon" version which was a nuclear depth bomb. *Thor* was produced from 1952-68 and used by both Services.

*** Hank Zeile spent his life working on nuclear power projects in support of national security and describes the evolution of nuclear power during the Cold War years in "The Nuclear Weapons Debate" and "The Navy Goes Nuclear."**

The Nuclear Weapons Debate

The atomic bombs used to end the war with Japan, ***caused many of the technical luminaries whom Dr. Robert J. Oppenheimer***

---

[38] Jeremy Isaacs and Taylor Downing, *Cold War An Illustrated History, 1945-1991*, Little, Brown and Company, Boston 1998, p.149

[39] Harry S. Truman, op. cit., p. x

had gathered at Los Alamos to have second thoughts about having participated in the enterprise to develop such a devastating weapon. Oppenheimer, who managed the scientists at Los Alamos, also became emotionally troubled but, even after he left Los Alamos, he continued to be involved In high-level policy committees dealing with nuclear matters. There **he vigorously argued against America building more atomic bombs** (A-bombs), **especially against building a by far more powerful one—the hydrogen bomb (H-bomb).**

Dr. Edward Teller, who headed up the physics department at Los Alamos, early on had suggested that an even more powerful weapon could be built and lobbied Dr. Robert J. Oppenheimer to work on a weapon that **greatly boosted the explosive yield by fusing isotopes of hydrogen.** Eventually, **Oppenheimer relieved Teller** of his supervisory role and let him work on *'Teller's Super.'* It started out as Teller's Super but would have many name changes, eventually called a **thermonuclear bomb (H-bomb).**

So, when the Soviets exploded their first atomic bomb on **August 29,1949** it shocked our leaders in Washington. When it was confirmed that the Soviet Union had the bomb, **Lewis Strauss, Teller and Lawrence lobbied President Truman for a crash effort to build the H-bomb.** They correctly assumed that the Russians had all the American technical data on the II-bomb and could get there ahead of the United States. **The Joint Chiefs of Staff were also in agreement and added a military requirement for the H-bomb.**

The Atomic Energy Commission (AEC), however, had the lead for that decision and AEC commissioners were divided and couldn't come to unanimous decision. Its chairman, David Liebenthal, sided with his General Advisory Committee, headed by Oppenheimer. In Congress. the **Chairman of the Joint Committee on Atomic Energy, Senator McMahon, was convinced that war with the Soviet Union was inevitable and "wanted to blow them off the face of the earth before they did the same to us."** Shortly thereafter McMahon was diagnosed with cancer. But **from**

his hospital bed he sent a message to President Truman that he "would start impeachment hearings if "Mike" (another name for Teller's Super) was not built."

*By then **President Truman has chartered a committee** made up of the Secretary of State, Dean Acheson, Secretary of Defense Louis Johnson and the Chairman of the AEC to look into the advisability of building the H-bomb. When the three came in to brief the president he asked:*

"Can the Russians do it?" The answer was yes. The President said: "in that case we have no choice. We'll go ahead."[40] *A day after he made his decision the President was informed that **physicist Klaus Fuchs had been a Soviet spy while working at Los Alamos.** The damage assessment concluded that Fuchs had access to all the technical information about Mike. This set off a political firestorm in Washington.*

*The AEC facility at Hanford, Washington had been hastily built to supply the plutonium for the bomb that was dropped on Nagasaki. It was no longer up to the task to supply the weapons material (plutonium and tritium) in the quantities needed to build hydrogen bombs. **So the largest project ever undertaken by the United States was started —AEC's Savannah River Plant. It consisted of 5 huge reactors, facilities to fabricate fuel and target materials for the reactors, fuel reprocessing facilities, and heavy water plant** along with all the roads and infrastructure on a huge reservation near Aiken, South Carolina. In addition, a **new large weapons material production reactor was built at Hanford Washington—the N-Reactor**.*

*But these were not the only challenges the Truman Administration wrestled with. In **September 1949 the Chinese Communists won the Civil War and Mao Zedong and his cadre took over China.** Then on **June 25, 1950,** North Korean troops invaded South Korea. *Over the next two years United States defense budget quadrupled.**

*Now fast forward to **1979 as President Jimmy Carter** faced*

---

[40] David Milne (2015), Worldmaking, The Art and Science of American Diplomacy

another decision regarding nuclear weapons. Geopolitics was unravelling, not in our favor; Soviet Union invaded Afghanistan, our staunch ally, the Shah of Iran was deposed, and The Nuclear Weapons Council was concerned about **Soviet Union's huge nuclear weapons arsenal and our aging nuclear weapons materials production infrastructure.**

A joint Energy Research and Development Administration (ERDA, *the successor agency to AEC) and Department of Defense study group evaluated* **various scenarios to maintain America's arsenal as well as to increase it in case there was a 'break out' by the Soviet Union to increase its arsenal.** *The study group's* **"Starbird Report"** *recommended construction of up to 5 new weapons materials reactors along with the required infrastructure. The independent National Security Council evaluation agreed with the ERDA/DOD study.*

Towards the end of the Carter Administration, the President **authorized ERDA to start down the path of a major systems acquisition.** *When* **President Reagan, not a fan of nuclear weapons, took over, he put a hold on the New Production Reactor (NPR) program.** *Nonetheless, there was a critical need for the* **production of tritium, a radioactive isotope of hydrogen that decays with a 12.3-year half-life.** *Thus the* **tritium in the H-bombs has to be periodically replaced.** *In addition, the National Research Council evaluation of Department of Energy's (DOE, the successor agency to ERDA) weapons material production reactors found them unsafe and* **only one was permitted to operate at half power.**[41]

*For years US Government didn't know the cost of the Nuclear Weapons Program. In 1996, however, independently it was estimated that from 1940 to 1996 the total cost, in constant 1996 dollars, was 5,821 billion; second only to the total cost of the Social Security Program.[42]

---

[41] National Research Council (1987). *Safety Issues at the Defense Production Reactors* (A National Research Council Report to the Department of Energy). Washington D.C: National Academy Press.

[42] *Nuclear Notebook, Bulletin of Atomic Scientists* November/December, 1996

***Henriks (Hank) Zeile graduated from the United States Merchant Marine Academy Class of 1960 with a Bachelor of Science degree in Marine Engineering and holds a Master of Science degree in Engineering from Union College and a Master of Science degree in Management from the Rensselaer Polytechnic Institute.

After serving three years as an **engineer on a merchant ship**, he spent the next 15 years at the Knolls Atomic Power Laboratory (KAPL), where he supervised **Navy nuclear prototype plant** operations, training and qualification of Navy personnel, design verification testing, and refueling and plant modifications. Later, he served as S5G prototype plant manager, manager of nuclear plant design, manager of refueling and reactor servicing operations and managed KAPL's Windsor Connecticut Site.

During the next 14 years at the **Idaho National Laboratory**, he managed nuclear safety research, special energy programs, the power reactors department and Department of Energy's new production reactor program. Mr. Zeile spent the last 5 years of his career at Morrison Knudsen Corporation as Vice President of Government Operations where he had the corporate responsibility for major government-funded remediation and construction projects as well as the start-up of Rocky Mountain Remediation Services, L.L.C., to perform environmental **remediation of the Rocky Flats Environmental Test Site**. During the first 10 years in retirement he provided consulting services to national laboratories and Department of Energy contractors.

The government developed *Civil Defense* **drills** and education as a key priority in the new nuclear age. **In 1950, President Truman instituted the Federal Civil Defense Administration (FCDA) to organize Civil Defense groups across the US** to help Americans physically and psychologically prepare for--and potentially survive--a nuclear attack. The Eisenhower Administration practiced running the government after a nuclear attack with *Operation Alert* annual exercises. **We** *"Baby Boomers"* remember being taught to *"duck and cover"* during air raid drills in elementary school.

1961 after SL-1 reactor accident *Idaho National Engineering and Environmental Laboratory, INEEL 61-9*

Many Americans built fall-out shelters and the tough moral question then was **"Would you let your neighbors in during an attack?" Women bore a great share of the physical and mental stresses** of living under the threat of potential nuclear attacks during the Cold War; including everything from struggling with how talk to kids about the threat to figuring out civil defense food strategies to caring for children during a potential nuclear attack.

In 1953 the **Federal Civil Defense Administration** staged a civil defense 16 kiloton nuclear test exercise named *Operation Doorstep*. Two houses, eight bomb shelters, mannequins, and 50 cars were photographed after the test to show the effects. Soldiers participating in the Desert Rock V exercise were also photographed. **The surviving house 7,500 feet from the detonation had been strengthened with reinforcing steel bars!** *Operation Doorstep* results claimed that sheltering in fallout shelters and basements could enable survival from a nuclear blast and that **drivers should open their windows to help enable their survival!** These efforts were part of national efforts to reassure the public that they could survive nuclear war.[43]

---

[43] *Operation Doorstep* produced by Byron Inc, Washington DC 1953; www. PeriscopeFilm.com

Our neighbor was drafted in 1959 and after basic training was sent to Ft. Belvoir Virginia to work for the post engineer on base infrastructure. He remembers during 1960 sitting around the pool talking with his buddies about the future and families--with none of them wanting to be responsible for wives and kids during the tense atmosphere of potential nuclear war.

After the disintegration of the Soviet Union and the end of the Cold War in 1991, American civil defense planning and efforts were discontinued and forgotten. However, today with threats of terrorist dirty bombs and potential ICBM threats looming from North Korea, cities and regions are dusting-off Cold War civil defense programs and relooking at the lessons learned.

Los Angeles and Ventura County, California are trailblazers in renewed efforts to develop response plans and to educate their populations about how to react to a potential nuclear event. Dr. Alex Wellerstein, a nuclear weapons historian at the Stevens Institute, and others have started a nonprofit effort named *Reinventing Civil Defense* to educate Americans on nuclear threats.[44]

In January 2018, civil defense officials in Hawaii mistakenly set-off an alarm notifying hundreds of thousands that nuclear ballistic missiles were inbound which threw the entire state into panic, thereby setting-off a thorough review of alert procedures.

The Atomic Energy Commission started building **plutonium triggers** for nuclear bombs in 1953 at the **Rocky Flats Plant** (2 miles from our house) northwest of Denver. Fires in 1957 and 1969 (and a 1988 contamination incident) led to large-scale radioactive waste which necessitated one of the costliest environmental remediation efforts in US history. Author Kristen Iverson, who grew up near Rocky Flats, wrote, "Plutonium particles were found at elementary school 12 miles away. **There was plutonium and radioactive particles found throughout the Denver metro area.**"...."Part of the reason that there were no indictments was that it was argued that these were officials with the Department

---

[44] Ralph Vartabedian and W.J. Hennigan, Duck and cover 2.0: How North Korea is prompting new efforts to prepare for a nuclear attack, *Tribune Washington Bureau,* July 27, 2017

of Energy and Rockwell who were operating within instructions from the Department of Energy — that is, that these environmental violations were sort of OK because what is most important is the production of plutonium [parts for bombs]." [45]

NATO was shifting its defense strategies from conventional forces to more inexpensive atomic weapons. In 1953, President Eisenhower gave his *"Atoms For Peace"* speech to the UN General Assembly to reassure the public and to emphasize the peaceful uses of nuclear reactor power during a time of rapid build-up of atomic weaponry. Some excerpts from Eisenhower's speech:

"I feel impelled to speak today in a language that in a sense is new – one which I, who have spent so much of my life in the military profession, would have preferred never to use. That new language is the language of atomic warfare...

To the making of these fateful decisions, the United States pledges before you--and therefore before the world--its determination to help solve the fearful atomic dilemma--to devote its entire heart and mind to find the way by which the miraculous inventiveness of man shall not be dedicated to his death, but consecrated to his life."[46]

The **1956 *Federal Aid Highway Act*** provided financing for the ***Dwight D. Eisenhower National System of Interstate and Defense Highways*** which was planned to improve national security by connecting cities and military bases throughout the US. **The overpasses were specifically designed to be 17 feet high to accommodate the transport of strategic missiles on the interstate highways.**

Anti-Communism In 1950, retired General Eisenhower spearheaded the ***Crusade For Freedom*** campaign throughout the US to support ***Radio Free Europe*** and various anti-Communist efforts including construction of a *Freedom Bell* which was sent to Berlin as a symbol of American support. Congress had passed

[45] Iversen, Kristen, as quoted in NPR *Fresh Air* June 12, 2012 *"Under the Nuclear Shadow of Colorado's Rocky Flats;"* Full Body Burden, Growing Up in the Nuclear Shadow of Rocky Flats, New York, Crown Publishing Group 2013

[46] President Dwight D. Eisenhower, December 8, 1953, *Speech before the United Nations General Assembly*, New York

the *"Federal Employees Loyalty Program"* in 1947 which created boards to review political loyalty as the *Red Scare* intensified.

During the *"Red Scare,"* Constitutional protections were thrown aside as thousands of Americans were investigated by the House Un-American Activities Committee (HUAC) and the Senate Government Operations Committee Permanent Subcommittee on Investigations under Wisconsin **Senator Joe McCarthy's** aggressive investigations--finally ended in 1954.

1957 Daryl Phillippi and a photo F2H-2P *Banshee*
aboard *USS Saratoga* in the North Atlantic

Aircrewman Daryl Phillippi enlisted: "Right out of high school in 1956, at the age of 17, I joined the Navy with "boot camp" at Great Lakes.

*My decision was to go aviation and was sent to Norman, OK for Airman prep school prior to transfer to Pensacola FL for Photographers Mate School. Upon graduation I chose to be transferred to the **Light Photographic Squadron VFP-62 in Jacksonville, FL. This was the squadron credited with exposing the missiles in Cuba in 1962.** The squadron was tasked with **supporting the fleet with a detachment of 3 photo planes for each carrier.** The sea duty for the junior enlisted was mostly voluntary.*

*I had my first opportunity in **1957,** for a detachment on the*

USS Saratoga heading to the North Atlantic in support of **Operation Strikeback**. We were using **F2H-2P Banshees**. This was actually a **NATO operation and was comprised of 125 warships, the largest gathering of ships since D-Day.** Our task was to cross the Arctic Circle and then head south and evade the north-bound forces. The excitement of this cruise was enough to get me to volunteer for a **9-month 1958 Med cruise on the Saratoga**. Our mission was to photograph the harbors and to map the airfields that would be used as "diversionary fields" for aircraft that could not make it back to the carrier. **The time was long before satellites, so we were "the eyes of the fleet." They were fighter photo planes so we did the camera installation and set the controls and the pilots became the photographers.** On this deployment, we used **F9F-8P Cougars**.

My next deployment was in 1959, on the USS FD Roosevelt for 6 months in the Med with the **F8U-1P Crusaders.**

After all this exciting time, the enlistment was coming to an end with **President Eisenhower reducing the forces, so I mustered out.** *I then looked to affiliating with NARTU Norfolk as a Reserve. My older brother had also just mustered out and I convinced him to join me in looking at Norfolk. We lived in Pittsburgh so we had to be airlifted. He was Ltjg and had been a Rader Observer in VAW-12 flying AD5W Guppies off the USS Randolph.* **They had lost a crew in the Med and he was not up to flying again.** *I convinced him to "humor" his kid brother and at least go with me to check it out. We were assigned to VS-864. It was 1959 and this was a Reserve unit before the "one Navy" concept.* **VS-861 was called to active duty during the Cuban Crises call-up.** *VS-864 was the augmentation unit and about half the squadron was recalled.* **I had volunteered to take the place** *of the recalled Photo-mate as he had recently married and just started a new business.* **I was unemployed but was told, "No volunteers needed."**

Time passed and I took a 4-year break to serve an apprenticeship as a tool & die maker but returned to Norfolk after becoming a journeyman in 1967. In 1970, several of the aircrew heard about the opportunity to join a forming unit at NAS Pax River. There were three crews put together and we had a P-3 aircraft from NAS Moffit VP-91. We were designated as VP-91 Det Pax. Our first active duty was **spent off Bermuda where the regular Navy had lost contact with a Russian sub lurking around the area. Our crew of old S-2F folks made contact with the sub on the second day. This sort of cemented the USNR role as "pros."**

In Nov. 1970, VP-661 & 662 P-2 guys were integrated from NAS Andrews, and the unit **became VP-68, flying P3A aircraft, becoming the first Atlantic Fleet Naval Air Reserve squadron to do so. We were now part of the bigger picture and given "real tasks."** *Our first active duty was to NAF Lajes, Azores and then to Rota. During my time with VP-68, I became qualified for "inflight-cameraman" and received my aircrew wings."*

Chapter 5

Uprisings, Revolts and Nationalism against Soviet domination erupted in countries throughout Eastern Europe (and also within the USSR) were brutally put down with thousands imprisoned or fleeing. President Eisenhower noted in 1954 that, "From behind the Iron Curtain, there are **signs that tyranny is in trouble** and reminders that its structure is as brittle as its surface is hard."[47]

While the US and Allies mounted many anti-communist, campaigns including broadcasts from *Radio Free Europe, Voice of America,* and other means—there was little the West could do actually do to help, especially with strategic nuclear tensions so high. Unfortunately, the Voice of America gave Hungarians false impressions that the West might intervene when it never could, leading up to the disastrous 1956 Hungarian uprising.

Canada, the United States, and other Western nations did provide sanctuary for the thousands who managed to escape the repressive regimes. Victor Sebestyen notes that "...in the early 1950s **Hungary** lived under the most repressive dictatorship in the Eastern bloc...There was resentment against the Soviet Union in all the satellite countries after the war; Russia regarded them all as colonies and behaved towards them as such. But **nowhere was the hatred as strong and as deep as in Hungary....Hungary, under a fascist dictator of its own for two decades, had, unlike the Poles or the Czechs, invaded the Soviet Union in the Second World War.**[48]

---

[47] President Dwight D. Eisenhower, *State of the Union Address to Congress,* January 7, 1954

[48] Victor Sebestyen, *Twelve Days-Revolution 1956,* London; Phoenix-Orion Books Ltd. 2007. pp. xxv-xxvi

Throughout Eastern Europe, tens of thousands of extremely brave citizens rose up against Soviet domination and were brutally put down:

- 1953 East Germany strike
- 1956 uprising in Poznan, Poland; put down by 10,000 troops & 360 tanks[49]; over 74 protesters killed[50]
- 1956 Hungary (2600 killed, over 300 executed, many thousands imprisoned, tortured; over 200,000 fled the country)[51]
- 1962 Workers protest against Khrushchev's raising food costs & work quotas in Novocherkaask, Russia; over 110 casualties, many sent to *Gulags*[52]
- 1968 Prague; *Czech Spring*
- 1981 Poland *Solidarity* strike; Jaruzelski Martial Law; Lech Walesa and Catholic leaders led opposition
- 1989 Berlin, Eastern European border walls taken down

Nationalism and Communist Support America and its allies were fearful of the nationalist policies of **Egyptian Colonel Gamal Abdel Nasser** and the *Free Officers Movement* who took power in 1952. Nasser **nationalized the Suez Canal** on July 26, 1956 and **Britain, France, and Israel** secretly colluded and invaded Egypt on October 29th to retake the Suez Canal. **The Suez invasion gave the Soviet Union cover for its heavy military response to the Hungarian uprising during the same time. The Suez Crisis** demonstrated to regional nations the dangers of continuing Western *imperialism* and paved the way for increasing Soviet influence in the Middle East. President Eisenhower ended the British-French-Israeli attack and Canadian Prime Minister Lester Pearson won the Nobel Peace Prize for his efforts to descale the conflict and setting-up the first United Nations peace-keeping operation.

---

[49] *Grzegorz Ekiert; Jan Kubik (2001). Rebellious Civil Society : Popular Protest and Democratic Consolidation in Poland, 1989–1993. Ann Arbor: University of Michigan Press. pp. 27–29*

[50] *Maciej Szewczyk (2005). "Poznański czerwiec 1956"* Official figures

[51] Sebestyen, Ibid, pp. xxv-xxvi

[52] Vladislav Zubok and Constantine Pleshkov, Inside the Kremlin's Cold War: from Stalin to Khrushchev, Harvard University Press, p. 262

Correspondent Donald Neff observed, "From Washington's viewpoint, Nasser had become too successful, his prestige too high and his policies too independent. He represented basic penetration by the Soviet Union...On May 16, he recognized Communist China, the nation that Washington insisted on keeping out of the assemblies of the United Nations and with which it boycotted all trade. Washington feared that Saudi Arabia, Syria, and Yemen would soon follow.

The Russians were enjoying a surge of popularity throughout that part of the Arab world that was aligning itself **with Egypt's Nasser against Britain and its Baghdad Pact**...For the Arab countries, so long captive to the West's monopoly in the region, the appearance of an alternate benefactor was a heady experience."... ."**Suez was a hinge point in history**. It spelled the end of Western colonialism and the entry of America as the major Western power... Britain, France, and Israel, by colluding and waging an unprovoked war, displayed such contempt for justice and the rule of law that they badly blotched the West's record in its competition against Communism...The Soviet Union secured its presence in the Middle East after Suez....the **Russians now appear so embedded in the Middle East** that it seems unrealistic to suppose that any settlement of the region's continuing turmoil could occur without active Soviet support."[53]

---

[53] Donald Neff, *Warriors at Suez*, Linden Press/Simon & Schuster, New York 1981, pp. 253, 256-257, 438

Chapter 6
Evolution of Nuclear Deterrence and the Triad

Avro *Vulcan* Bombers (crew 5, range 2500
nm at 565 MPH, Mach .86) *Royal Air Force*

Initially, the US had a monopoly on nuclear weapons and concentrated on building-up strategic bomber forces until surprised by the Soviet nuclear test in 1949. In the 1950s, both superpowers worked to develop much more powerful **Hydrogen (thermonuclear fusion) bombs**. The US tested it in November 1952 followed closely by a successful Soviet test in August 1953. During the 1950s, the US embarked on accelerated nuclear bomb-building programs, eventually constructing about one bomb a day to build up the nuclear arsenal.

During the 44 years of the Cold War, the US, Allies, and the USSR developed deterrence doctrines to keep the other side from using nuclear weapons since both sides knew they could also be destroyed (**Mutual Assured Destruction-MAD**). The US, Allies, our professional counterparts in the Soviet Union and the Warsaw Pact created vital stability by building organizations of highly-trained professionals and procedures to handle, support, maintain, and defend against nuclear weapons. In addition to manned bombers, in the late 1950s, the US and USSR both developed **Intercontinental Ballistic Missiles (ICBMs)** hardened in underground siloes to survive attacks. In 1958, F.E. Warren AFB outside Cheyenne Wyoming became the first operational ICBM base with crews manning 24 *Atlas* missiles.

In the early 1960s, both sides began to deploy **Submarine-Launched Ballistic Missiles (SLBMs)**. Since submarines were constantly moving requiring their positions to be updated, early submarine inertial navigation systems (INS) were not as accurate as those in fixed silo ICBMs. Navy ASW forces--including VP—complemented submarines whose mobility and stealth became increasingly important to the US strategic nuclear deterrence **Triad** along with **B-52 bombers** and **ICBMs**. Britain operated nuclear delivery **"V bombers"** and *Polaris*-armed submarines and France had nuclear delivery systems and extensive nuclear reactor engineering experience.

Eventually in the late 1970s and 1980s, the USSR and US fielded **mobile short and intermediate range nuclear delivery systems** became operational and increased the difficulties of detection.

Strategic Bombers From 1947 to the late 1950s, US deterrence was primarily based on *the Strategic Air Command (SAC)* initially flying nuclear-armed B-36s and B-47s, and later B-52s around the clock--along with some Navy carrier-based air delivery capabilities. General Curtis LeMay built up SAC in the mid-1950s to about *2,000 bombers* (B-47s and B-52s), *800 tankers*, and *radar early warning radar stations*. SAC also trained in low altitude flying on *"Oil Burner routes"* in the US to try to avoid Soviet SAMs in an actual attack. **B-52s could be airborne in less than 15 minutes according to**

bomber veterans' remembrances.[54]

*When asked at a 1957 briefing how his bombers would be able to transit to the USSR to bomb if a launch was eminent and whether it was national policy, **SAC General Curtis LeMay** said, *"I will know from my own intelligence whether or not the Russians are massing their planes...for a massive attack against the United States. If I come to that conclusion, I'm going to knock the s_t out of them before they get off the ground...No it's not national policy, but it's my policy."*[55]

In 1960 the Air Force began flying nuclear-capable *Hound Dog* Air-Launched Cruise Missiles (ALCMs) on B-52s. The *Hound Dog* was a "stand-off" weapon that extended the offensive nuclear capabilities of the B-52 to enable destruction of Soviet air defense sites.

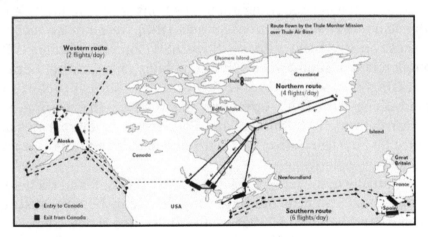

1966 *Chrome Dome* Routes *USAF*

From 1960 until a crash in Greenland in 1968, the **USAF maintained 12 nuclear-armed B-52s airborne at all times. These *"Chrome Dome"* missions included flights to the north of Alaska, Canada, Greenland, and near Western Europe.** SAC also maintained a continuous airborne EC-135 (Boeing 707 variant) command post from 1961-1991 to provide control

---

[54] http://b52stratofortressassociation.yuku.com/topic/53/Cold-War-alert#.
WUfilYWcHHo

[55] WGBH *Interview with Robert Sprague,* Tape #C03005, p.4

in case SAC headquarters was destroyed in a first strike. After 1968, B-52s were maintained on "High Alert" near runways until President George H.W. Bush ended these alerts in 1991 as the Soviet Union fell apart.

Talk to any SAC veteran and you will hear all about the extremely strict testing standards and the stresses of alerts and ORIs (snap Operational Readiness Inspections) on bomber & ICBM crews and their families. The 1955 movie *"Strategic Air Command"* starring Jimmy Stewart as a recalled Reserve B-47 pilot has a lot of footage of 1950s SAC operations.

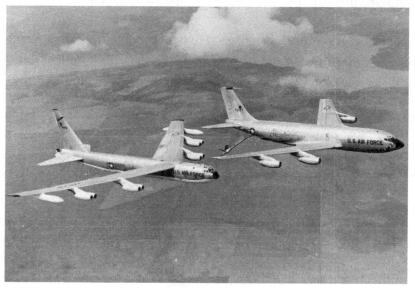

KC-135(crew 3-4, cruise 11,000 nm at 530 MPH) and a B-52D *USAF*

*Steve Raymond remembers his time as a KC-135 tanker pilot in the early 1970s:

"Independence Day—more commonly known these days as Fourth of July—has always been an important holiday to me...On July 4, 1973, I was assigned to Kadena Air Base on Okinawa as the copilot of a KC-135 crew that was sent there in support of Operation Bullet Shot at the tail end of the Southeast Asian conflict. My contributions to this effort in particular and to the defense of the United States in general were pretty inconsequential and not very

life threatening compared to the ordeals of many others. However, among many benefits, my military experience provided me with first hand exposure to other parts of the world—underdeveloped and unfriendly places where the people are less free and have fewer opportunities than we have in the U.S. These experiences greatly enhanced my appreciation for our country, its history, and the many advantages of living here. Wherever I have been in the world since then, I always feel something between gratitude and relief when I return home......A very important and consistent part of our combined 4th of July celebration every year has been our reading of the Declaration of Independence, usually at breakfast time."

***Steve Raymond graduated from the School of Operations Research and Information Engineering (ORIE) at Cornell University, trained as an Air Force tanker pilot, and was stationed at Blytheville AFB Arkansas. He is President of Raymond Handling Concepts in California.

*Former bomber pilot Dino Atsalis remembers SAC Alerts and deterrence in the 1980s:

*"Spanning some four decades, support for the United States **TRIAD strategic nuclear operational assets** came from the Navy ballistic submarine force, a launch platform for submarine-launched ballistic missiles (SLBMs) patrolling the Earth's oceans undetected, working in partnership with the Air Force's land-based intercontinental ballistic missiles (ICBMs) based in the heartland of the continental United States, and strategic manned-bombers based in the United States. USAF strategic bombers and intercontinental ballistic missiles were assigned to Strategic Air Command (SAC) headquartered at **Offutt AFB** in Omaha Nebraska.*

*To give an idea of the magnitude of our strategic bomber deterrent, **between 1980-1993 SAC Bomber Wings** were located at FB-111A Bases: Pease AFB, NH and Plattsburgh AFB, NY; B-52 (G or H Model) Wings were located at Andersen AFB Guam, Castle AFB CA, March AFB, CA, Mather AFB CA, Fairchild AFB WA, Minot AFB ND, Grand Forks AFB ND, Ellsworth AFB SD,*

Dyess AFB TX, Carswell AFB TX, Blytheville AFB AR, Barksdale AFB LA, K.I. Sawyer AFB MI, Wurtsmith AFB MI, Seymour Johnson AFB NC, Griffiss AFB NY, and Loring AFB ME. I flew B-52Gs at Loring AFB and volunteered for FB-111As at Pease AFB.[56]

USAF bomber aircraft on alert in support of the **Single Integrated Operational Plan (SIOP)** *meant a SAC assigned crews would spend a week at the alert facility located at their base of assignment. During the 1980s, at most SAC bases across the United States, B-52 and FB-111 crews assumed alert on Thursday morning, ate and slept at the alert facility for a week and then relieved the following Thursday morning. The alert facility was collocated near the alert force aircraft parked at an end of the base's operational runway that was usually more than two miles in length.*

A typical Bomb Wing's alert force usually consisted of four B-52s and eight KC-135 tankers. For a Bomb Wing of FB-111s, there were usually six FB-111s and six KC-135 tankers. Depending on the location of the active duty Air Force alert tanker force, it was augmented by Air National Guard KC-135s collocated at the same base or at an Air National Guard base in the same region of the United States.

A SAC crew was considered an integral crew; crew members flew peacetime training missions together, completed ground training and sat SIOP alert together; in other words, did everything together. A B-52 crew of six was comprised of the Aircraft Commander, Co-Pilot, Radar Navigator, Navigator, Electronic Weapons Officer and Gunner. For a FB-111 crew, the integral crew of two comprised of the Aircraft Commander and the Radar Navigator. Working as a team, a well-coordinated and trained integral SAC bomber crew, six or two-man crew, could drop bombs on target inside a circular error probability (CEP) of 100 feet (radius). This targeting criterion was regularly met well before the space-based GPS navigation systems were established.

Day one of alert, Thursday, was usually the busiest day for a crew assuming alert duty. Flying gear and personal gear were brought to the alert facility by 0800. The daily alert briefing was

---

[56] SAC Bomber bases, https://en.wikipedia.org/wiki/Strategic_Air_Command

attended by both the on-going bomber and tanker crews while the off-going bomber and tanker crews retrieved their flying gear from the aircraft. **The daily alert briefing included; a weather brief for operations from the SAC base to the Soviet Union, operational, maintenance and communications updates and the USSR ballistic missile time of flight that could impact the status and reaction time of bomb wing's alert force.**

B-52 Alert Crew (Crew 5, cruise 10,000 nm at 525 MPH) USAF via Ryan Crierie www.alternatewars.com

Following the daily brief, crews met at the vehicle assigned to a crew for the week; quad cab pick-up for a B-52 crew or a two-door pick-up for a FB-111 crew, to head out to the assigned alert aircraft. Arriving at the aircraft, the bomber crew always ensured they were in compliance with the Air Force two-man policy for aircraft loaded with nuclear weapons. **The crew would first enter the aircraft to stow their gear and confirm switch positions for aircraft and weapon systems that would allow for a quick start of the aircraft and allow the crew to get the aircraft off the ground in minimum time. Once the interior inspection was complete the crew then completed the aircraft weapons inventory inspection.**

For the B-52; the **nuclear weapon inventory** *usually had* **eight short-range attack missiles (SRAM) and four gravity weapons (bombs), ready to arm once inflight.** *For the FB-111; the*

*weapons compliment consisted of **two SRAMs and two gravity weapons**. Once the weapon inventory was complete, the crew buttoned up the aircraft and departed for ground training; target study for their sortie's specific targets; 12 for the B-52 and 4 for the FB-111, followed by communications and operations training and testing.*

*For the rest of the week, during normal duty hours, ground training and additional duty assignments were completed. If there was an aircraft simulator collocated at the bomb wing, **crews would participate in 5-hour simulator training sessions once or twice during the week of alert.** Weekends were usually free, where family could meet with their loved one on alert at family center near the alert facility or at the respective officers or enlisted club. Alert crew members could attend social activities and athletic events on base. This took some coordination amongst the crew as there was only one vehicle to share between a crew of six (B-52) or two (FB-111). Many times, if one or more members of different crews would share one vehicle as appropriate.*

The alert force facility was located in a remote high security area providing for separate or shared bedrooms, bath and shower facilities, a dining facility, work-out area, library, and entertainment area; television and movies. If the alert force was confined to the alert facility, the facility could provide the alert force crewmembers everything needed for a daily routine when the alert force was put in a restricted status.

***If the alert force was in a restricted status**, that meant the crews were confined to the alert facility itself. The crews could not travel outside the perimeter of the high security area. This allowed for minimum travel time from the facility to the bomber aircraft. The restricted status was usually due to the position of the **Soviet ballistic missile submarines**, where missile flight time calculated using the worst-case scenario would require the alert bomber and tanker force to take-off in minimum time in advance of an arriving sub launched missile. At times, bomber aircraft were repositioned closer to the end of the runway to minimize even more the time to get the aircraft of the ground.*

Worst-case scenario would have bomber and tanker crews at the aircraft ready to start engines and takeoff at a moments notice.

The missions of the Navy's P-3 surveillance aircraft played an integral role that affected the readiness status of USAF bomber aircraft on alert in support of the Single Integrated Operational Plan (SIOP). *Around the clock vigilance by the Navy's P-3 aircraft surveillance force provided valuable information for the National Command Authorities (NCA) to allow the strategic bomber alert force to maintain the highest level of response for their assigned nuclear deterrence mission.* **If the P-3 force made contact in certain geographic areas of the Earth's oceans with a Soviet ballistic missile submarine, or lost contact with a Soviet submarine in these geographic areas, this affected the readiness status of the strategic bomber alert force.**

***Captain Dino Atsalis is a St Michaels College graduate, class 1979, received his commissioned as a Second Lieutenant through AFROTC. Following graduation, he attended Air Force Undergraduate Pilot Training at Reese AFB, Lubbock, TX, Class 81-03, then attended B-52G qualification training at Castle AFB CA, and was assigned to the 69th Bomb Squadron, 42nd Bomb Wing at Loring AFB, ME. He flew as a co-pilot from October 1981 to December1984, deploying to Moron AFB, Spain in Fall 1983 for a joint NATO training exercise, and then volunteered for assignment to the FB-111A from January 1985 to September 1987. Following qualification training at Plattsburgh AFB, NY, he was assigned to the historic 393rd Bomb Squadron, 509th Bomb Wing at Pease AFB, NH. Deploying to Maple Flag, Cold Lake, Canada and the United Kingdom for joint NATO training exercises. He joined Delta Air Lines in August 1987 and currently flies as an Airbus A-330 Captain at JFK International Airport, NY. As an active pilot volunteer of the Air Line Pilots Association, Intl, Captain Atsalis has served as Boston local council First Officer representative; Chairman, Delta Master Executive Council Government Affairs Committee; and is a current member to the ALPA-PAC Steering Committee. Captain Atsalis resides with his family in Exeter, NH.

Chapter 7
Missiles and Air Defense

Distant Early Warning Line radar (The Air National Guard *Boys from Schenectady* specialized in ski C-130s resupply) *USAF*

To augment the *DEW Line* defenses, the **Navy maintained "barrier forces"** in the Northern Atlantic and Pacific comprised of 12 Destroyer Escorts and 16 converted *Liberty* ship radar pickets. The WV-2s (Lockheed Constellation airborne radar aircraft; also called EC-121s) flew up to 14-hour missions. To protect against Soviet attack, the US and Canada formed the **North American Air Defense Command (NORAD)** in 1957 as a joint command with headquarters at Peterson AFB Colorado and CFB Winnipeg Manitoba. Initially, the US and Canada both operated the Air Force's new Semi-Automatic Ground Environment (SAGE) air defense system. SAGE utilized the largest computer of its time, the 250-ton Q-7 command and control computer (created by MITs Lincoln Lab and built by IBM) which had **tens of thousands of vacuum tubes** and was operated in twin units for back-up reliance.[57]

---

[57] Ulmann B. (2014) *AN/FSQ-7: the computer that shaped the Cold War.* de Gruyter Oldenbourg, 2014. pp.179-181

WV-2 /EC-121 (Crew of 22, up to 20-hour missions, range 3,700 nm at 222 kts cruise) & *USS Sellstom (DER-255*; crew 209, speed 21 kts) Destroyer Escort; *Mahlon.K. Miller US Navy via vpnavy.com*

NORAD controlled both fighter aircraft and missile (initially *BOMARC* and *Nike*) interceptor units in the US and Canada. An extensive underground command and control bunker was constructed at **CFB North Bay Ontario** and began NORAD duties in 1963.

1961 RCAF CF-100 (crew 2, range 2,000 miles, speed 550 MPH) Alert *Canadian Department of National Defence*

Surface-to-Air Missiles (SAMs) with nuclear capability were developed by both superpowers to shoot down incoming aircraft. Conventional SAMs were used to shoot down Captain Gary Power's U-2 over Russia in 1960 and would play a crucial role in the defense of Hanoi during the Vietnam War. The Boeing **BOMARC** was an unsuccessful nuclear-capable SAM interceptor which was deployed in the US and Canada in the 1960s. The US Army developed many missiles such as the **Nike** series to provide air defense at over 200 sites around key cities, SAC bomber and ICBM bases, and some nuclear industrial sites.

1958 *Miss BOMARC*
www.nsarchive.gwu.edu/nukevault/

The Missile Race After Stalin's death in 1953, Nikita Khrushchev consolidated power and embarked on reforms and concentrated on developing strategic rocket and tactical missile capabilities.

Sergei Khrushchev, the Soviet leader's son who was a missile engineer, wrote that "We actually were the first to begin testing intercontinental missiles. **We were twelve to eighteen months ahead there and several months ahead in medium-range missiles.** The reason is very simple: we were in a great hurry while they were not. **The intercontinental ballistic missile was the Soviet Union's last hope for parity in the arms race...It was**

given the highest priority for resources. At a call from the chief designer, the seemingly impossible could be accomplished. The Americans were making progress without hurrying. According to their strategic concept, missiles, no matter what their range, **only supplemented aviation (bombers)**....The problem (of precise targeting) could only be solved by satellite. They would link continents and determine the exact location of targets, large and small."[58]

In 1956, Khrushchev threatened Western diplomats stating that *"We will bury you"* and in 1957 bragged that the Soviet Union had "all the rockets it needed."

The Soviets concentrated on building large rockets which could lift massive payloads. In May 1957, they launched the first ICBM in the world, the R-7, which became militarily operational in 1959. R-7 variants were used to launch *Sputnik* **in 1957** and for later space efforts. Sergei Khrushchev observed that "The kilograms and tons lifted into orbit (by Soviet rockets) were impressive and provoked a great deal of speculation. Complicated conclusions were drawn. Intelligence agents risked their lives trying to ferret out the secret to his astonishing success. The answer was in plain sight: the **backwardness of our technology, especially our instruments. They were heavy and bulky**. Because they were unreliable, they required one or two back-up systems. And all this added more and more weight. The poor degree of accuracy made a more powerful explosion necessary. The R-7 was the first Soviet missile adapted to a 5.5-ton thermonuclear warhead....The takeoff weight of the R-7 was almost **280 tons**. The American intercontinental Atlas rocket, which was designed to perform the same type of tasks, **weighed 1/3 of that.**"[59]

Khrushchev favored missiles over conventional forces, and suggested that the savings from military spending could be transferred to reform and improve the Soviet economy for the people. This philosophy made many enemies in the Soviet military-industrial complex and eventually contributed to his

---

[58] Sergei N. Khrushchev, *Nikita Khrushchev*, University Park PA, The Pennsylvania State University Press, 2000, pp. 263-264

[59] Khrushchev, Ibid., pp. 264-265

being removed from power; in 1958, "He (Khrushchev) felt that there should only be a **minimum of strategic aviation...Ballistic missiles could perform all of their functions**...(His) 'mistakes' in underestimating the role of aviation, artillery, a surface fleet, tanks, and much else began to be 'corrected' in 1964, immediately after his removal from power."[60]

The Soviet *Strategic Rocket Forces (SRF)* were created in 1959 as a special elite unit which had the priority to choose the most talented and promising personnel for its ranks. SRF personnel were highly motivated, patriotic, and the academic elite of the Soviet military and were given specialized training and responsibilities for **strategic land** missile operations; the Soviet Navy controlled maritime missiles.

Inter Continental Ballistic Missiles By the late 1950s, both SAC and the Soviets were developing ICBMs, eventually manned by crews in underground siloes, which became the main deterrent due their survivability and improved targeting accuracy. Early ICBMs were targeted for area and city destruction; as guidance capability technologies improved in both the US and USSR, ICBMs could be used for more precise targeting.

ICBM Close-calls Averted by Professionals

Both US and Soviet missile and air defense operators acted professionally and rationally to keep many incidents from escalating during the Cold War:

In October 1960, NORAD went to maximum alert when an early warning radar at Thule, Greenland, reported "that it had detected dozens of Soviet missiles launched against the United States...**The United States later determined that the radar had been fooled by the moonrise over Norway and computers misinterpreted this as an all-out attack on the United States.** Fortunately, the Soviet leader Nikita Khrushchev was in New York at the time, raising doubts that the attack was real." [61]

---

[60] Khrushchev, Ibid., pp. 300-301

[61] Eric Schlosser, *Command and Control: Nuclear weapons, the Damascus accident, and the Illusion of safety* (New York: Penguin Press, 2013), pp. 253–254)

A Soviet Hero in the ICBM Cold War

In the 1980s, the *Trident D5* SLBMs provided such increased accuracy, combined with stealth and mobility that the Soviets feared a potential **"decapitation strike"** by the US which motivated them to create **"Systema Perimetr"** or the **"Dead Hand"** nuclear control system to enable a Second Strike-back capability. [62]

In September 1983, **Soviet Air Defense Forces Lieutenant Colonel Stanislav Petrov** was on watch at a missile early-warning command center outside Moscow when computer alarms warned of 5 incoming Minuteman missiles. He made the momentous **decision to hold-off notifying his superiors, who might have ordered a retaliatory strike,** and tried to process the increasing information since he had a gut feeling that it might be a false computer-generated alarm. Petrov was later forced to resign for not carrying out standing orders.

*From Lieutenant Colonel Stanislav Petrov's New York Times Obituary:

*"As the computer systems in front of him changed their alert from "launch" to "missile strike," and insisted that the reliability of the information was at the "highest" level, Colonel Petrov had to figure out what to do....The estimate was that **only 25 minutes would elapse between launch and detonation**...As the tension in the command center rose — as many as 200 pairs of eyes were trained on Colonel Petrov — he made the decision to report the alert as a system malfunction.*

*"The false alarm was apparently set off when the **satellite mistook the sun's reflection off the tops of clouds for a missile launch**. The computer program that was supposed to filter out such information had to be rewritten. Colonel Petrov said the system had been rushed into service in response to the United States' introduction of a similar system. He said he knew it was not 100 percent reliable. Cold War tensions persisted.*

In November 1983, NATO carried out Able Archer 83, a big military exercise simulating a coordinated nuclear attack. The exercise,

---

[62] https://en.wikipedia.org/wiki/Dead_Hand_(nuclear_war)

alongside the arrival in Europe of Pershing II nuclear missiles, **led some in the Soviet leadership to believe that the United States was using it as a cover for war; the Soviets placed air units in East Germany and Poland on alert.**"[63]

1964 this B-52H crew survived windshear *USAF*

Bomber and ICBM Casualties, Accidents & Incidents

- In April 1950, a B-29 crashed into a mountain in New Mexico with one nuclear weapon aboard; **13** killed.
- Between 1959-1968 **Six B-52s** *with nuclear weapons crashed in Kentucky, North Carolina, California, Maryland, Spain, and Greenland.* Commenting the **1961 Goldsboro NC** accident, Defense Secretary Robert McNamara said that **"By the slightest margin of chance, literally the failure of two wires to cross, a nuclear explosion was averted."**[64]
- In October 1959, a KC-135 tanker and a B-52F with 2 nuclear weapons collided over Kentucky and crashed, **8** killed.
- In January 1966, a KC-135 tanker and a B-52G bomber

[63] *Stanislav Petrov, Soviet Officer Who Helped Avert Nuclear War, Is Dead at 77,* by Sewell Chan, New York Times Sept. 18, 2017 https://www.nytimes.com/2017/09/18/world/europe/stanislav-petrov-nuclear-war-dead.html?mcubz=0

[64] Center for Defense Information 1981; McNamara et al. 1963, p. 2). Center for Defense Information. 1981. *U.S. nuclear weapons accidents: Danger in our midst.* The Defense Monitor X(5) http://docs.nrdc.org/nuclear/files/nuc_81010001a_n22.pdf

carrying 4 hydrogen bombs collided and exploded; while the hydrogen bombs did not go off, there was widespread radioactive contamination near **Palomares, Spain**; one of the hydrogen bombs was not found in the sea for 80 days; **7** crewmen were killed.

- In January 1968, a fire on a B-52G caused the crew to eject and it crashed on the **Greenland icecap near Thule** with 4 hydrogen bombs; while the bombs did not detonate, there was radioactive damage; **1** member of the crew was killed.[65]
- **53** men were killed in an *Atlas II* repair accident in Searcy, AR in August 1965
- In 1980, in Damascus, AR Air Force personnel dropped 8 lb. socket 80 feet which initiated a massive Titan II fuel leak and an Airman was killed during remediation attempts.

Air Defense Accidents and Casualties
- In 1958, a US Army *Nike* missile exploded in New Jersey and killed **10**
- In January 1961, **2** Army technicians and **a** Navy *Seabee* were killed in Idaho during an explosion and meltdown of *Stationary Low Power Reactor (SL-1),* a small 3-megawatt Army experimental nuclear reactor being developed to power remote sites such as DEW line radar stations.
- In 1960 NORAD maximum alert when Thule Greenland early warning radar reported *"detected dozens of Soviet missiles-determined radar fooled by moonrise"*
- In 1961, the failure of an AT&T switch cut communications between SAC and NORAD and early warning radars which made SAC think an attack was taking place, so it ordered the entire B-52 alert force to ready for takeoff [66]
- Command & Control failures occurred in Colorado, Wyoming & New Jersey due to bad switches, computer

---

[65] Taagholt, Jørgen, and Hansen, Jens Claus. 2001. *Greenland: Security Perspectives.* Translator Daniel Lufkin. Fairbanks, Alaska: Arctic Research Consortium of the United States. p. 42
[66] Schlosser, Op. Cit., p. 286

chips and circuit cards, false alerts, and human error

- The Soviet *Strategic Rocket Forces,* Naval, and other forces also experienced numerous close-calls ***It is a tribute to both US and Soviet operators that their rational and professional actions kept many nuclear incidents from escalating.***

Chapter 8
Cold War Primer continued:
the 1960s-1980s

The Space Race was the long-term Cold War competition between the superpowers to gain the lead in rockets, satellites, guidance systems, and high-tech developments to dominate space. Space was the ultimate defense frontier and whoever dominated the "high ground" would have military advantages.

With the Soviets 1957 launch of *Sputnik* and their successful test of an ICBM, the *R-7*, the US redoubled its efforts to *close the Missile Gap* with the USSR. Fears abounded across the US about potential nuclear strikes on civilians and the government developed civil defense programs, drills, and information on how to stock fallout shelters, detect, and survive radiation.

In 1958, President Eisenhower established the *National Aeronautics and Space Administration (NASA)* to direct US space efforts and Congress passed the *National Defense Education Act* to rapidly stimulate science, mathematics, and technology education in high schools and colleges. There was a national urgency to catch-up and get ahead of the Russians in the *Space Race* which was critical for the national defense of the US. The Soviets had bragged that they were turning out *"rockets like sausages,"* but in reality, they only had several operational ICBMs in 1960.

We Baby Boomers remember this time and the sudden interest in outer space and the emphasis on "Modern Math," computers, and the sciences from elementary school up through high schools and college.

CORONA was the codename for the first American **spy satellite** operated by the CIA and the Air Force from 1959-1972 which photographed swaths of the USSR and China. *CORONA* films were ejected from the satellite, descended by parachute, and recovered by aircraft outfitted with unique catchers. The *CORONA* satellites initially complemented the U-2 spy plane and took on vastly increased roles after Captain Gary Power's U2 was shot-down over Russia in 1960.

C-119 (crew 5, range 1540 nm at 174 kts cruise)
recovering *CORONA* satellite film *USAF*

NASA embarked on a rapid program to screen candidates for the new *Mercury* manned space program to beat the Soviets in space. To meet NASA's selection criteria, a candidate had to be: a military test pilot with an engineering degree, maximum age of 40, max weight 180 lbs. and max height 5' 11" (to fit the existing 72" diameter *Redstone* and *Atlas* booster rockets). From an initial pool of 502 candidates, NASA narrowed the field down to the *"Mercury Seven"* comprised of married men aged 32-37; three had won the Distinguished Flying Cross, three were Navy, three Air Force, one was a Marine; and all came from small towns or cities.

An example of the *Astronauts'* superb physical strength, conditioning, and stamina is this excerpt from **Scott Carpenter's** letter to his wife, Rene: *"Just finished our first rides on the 'wheel'.... The **16-G rides today** after 3 days' practice were easier than the first day's 9-G rides, and dizziness afterwards."*[67] **(*Note: Being able to withstand 16 Gs in a 1959 centrifuge ride is an absolutely phenomenal physical ability).**

---

[67] Carpenter, Cooper, Glenn, Grissom, Schirra, Shepard, Slayton; *We Seven,* New York, Simon & Schuster 1962

Sergei Korolev, the chief designer of the Soviet space program who had barely survived 6 years in a Stalin prison, created the *Cosmonaut* program and determined candidate requirements: "25 --30 years old, no taller than 1.75 meters (5'7"), and weigh no more than 72 kilograms (159 lbs)."[68] ...."Unlike NASA's astronaut group, this group did not particularly consist of experienced pilots; **Belyayev was the most experienced with 900 flying hours.** The Soviet spacecraft were more automated than the American counterparts, so significant piloting experience was not necessary."[69]

In April 1961, the Soviets launched **Yuri Gagarin** into *earth orbit*, making him the first human in space. Gagarin had studied tractor engineering before becoming an Air Force jet pilot, was the most popular among his *Cosmonaut* peers, and was 5'2" which was an advantage in the small ***Vostok I (East)*** space capsule. His words just before launch *"Let's go!"* became a rallying cry throughout the Soviet world.[70]

*Rich Passamaneck joined NASA's Caltech Jet Propulsion Laboratory (JPL) in 1965 and served there until 1976.

Over an intense 3-year period, he worked on manual mathematical calculations to model the entry of a future NASA probe to Jupiter through various fields and belts to enable the mission's success. Rich says JPL operated three state-of-the-art IBM 7094 computers at the Space Flight Operations Facility which filled-up various rooms. Before joining JPL, Rich played several seasons as a minor league baseball catcher. He earned his PhD in Aerospace Engineering from the University of Southern California in the early Seventies and later taught Mechanical Engineering for many years at Colorado School of Mines.

In May 1961 **Alan Shepard** rode the *Mercury* capsule to become America's first astronaut in space and in February 1962 **John Glenn** became the *first American to orbit the earth* in *Friendship 7.* In 1961, President Kennedy had promised to land a man on the

---

[68] *Asif. A. Siddiqi 2000 Challenge to Apollo: The Soviet Union and the Space Race, 1945-1974. NASA, p.244*

[69] Siddiqi, Ibid, *p.246*

[70] *Rex Hall, David Shayler May 18, 2001, The Rocket Men: Vostok & Voskhod, the first Soviet manned spaceflights. Springer, p.150*

moon before 1970 and the *Apollo* program accomplished that mission in July 1969.

1960-1963 Tense Years in the Cold War

1960 Khrushchev inspecting *U-2* wreck *CIA*

In May 1960 the Soviets shot down **Captain Gary Power's U-2** as he photographed Russian installations and put him on a show trial with an accompanying propaganda barrage. The Central Intelligence Agency (CIA) trained Cuban exiles for the failed April 1961 *Bay of Pigs* invasion of Cuba and Fidel Castro increased military, political, and economic relations with the Soviet Union. In May 1961, President Kennedy sent Army **Special Forces "A Teams" to Vietnam** to train and bolster the South Vietnamese against Viet Cong guerrilla operations.

In August 1961, as the East Germans started building the **Berlin Wall to close off the eastern part of the city** and Secretary General Khrushchev tested America's young President Kennedy who reacted quickly to reinforce Berlin. Both superpowers racheted up their conventional and nuclear confrontation and deployed tanks and troops along the new Berlin Wall, increased defense readiness, and reinforced frontiers.

Roswell Gilpatric, the Deputy Secretary of Defense, emphasized stated America's resolve, "We have responded immediately with our Western Allies by reinforcing our garrisons in that beleaguered city. We have **called up some 150,000 reservists, increased**

our draft calls and extended the service of many who are in uniform....Our confidence in our ability to deter Communist action, or resist blackmail, is based upon a sober appreciation of the relative military power of the two sides. The fact is that this nation has a nuclear retaliatory force of such lethal power that any enemy move that it brought it into play would be an act of self-destruction on his part....Our forces are so deployed and protected that a sneak attack could not effectively disarm us.... The United States does not seek to resolve disputes by violence. But if forceful interference with our rights and obligations should lead to violent conflict—**as it well might**—the United States does not intend to be defeated"[71]

After the Soviets blockaded Berlin, President Kennedy made a speech on television and initiated nation-wide efforts to build **fallout shelters** since we appeared to be on the brink of nuclear war. He stated "In the event of an attack, the lives of those families which are not hit in a nuclear blast and fire can still be saved if they can be warned to take shelter and if that shelter is available.... We owe that kind of insurance to our families and to the country... The time to start is now. In the coming months, I hope to let every citizen know what steps he can take without delay to protect his family in case of attack. I know you would not want to do less."[72]

Tensions escalated rapidly as both superpowers and their allies built-up their forces and placed them on high alert, but eventually both sides eased-back. Valentin Falin, the former Soviet Ambassador to West Germany noted, "I would say that **in October 1961 the world was closer to the third world war than ever**...Our tanks were then positioned in Berlin, combat ready, **two hundred meters from American tanks.** And as an immediate participant in these events, let me assure you that if the Americans would follow the orders given to them—and the orders were to destroy the Berlin Wall—our tanks would then open fire." [73]

---

[71] Roswell L. Gilpatric, October 21, 1961 speech to the *Business Council*-Hot Springs, VA; *"Our Real Strength," Time* October 27, 1961

[72] President Kennedy, July 25, 1961 *televised speech to the nation*

[73] WGBH *interview with Valentin Falin. Tape* #89, side A, pp. 1-2

1962 A P-3 on patrol during the Navy
blockade in the *Cuban Missile Crisis US Navy*

President Kennedy initiated a successful naval blockade of Cuba in October 1962 to prevent the Soviets from completing installation of nuclear missiles. The USSR attempted to deploy three Strategic Rocket Forces regiments of **R-12 Medium Range missiles** (1200 miles range) and two regiments of **R-14 Intermediate Range missiles** (2200 miles) to Cuba along with patrol boats, fighters, anti-aircraft, armor, and troop reinforcements. Khrushchev and the Soviet military made this deployment in response to the US installing about 100 **Jupiter missiles in Turkey** and Italy in 1961. Part of the resolution of the Cuban missile crisis was the US commitment to remove the *Jupiter* sites in Turkey.

Americans were glued to television and radio sets as President Kennedy addressed the nation about the need to prepare for potential war as the crisis escalated. *Many Americans flooded to churches and formed lines for confession in Washington DC and throughout the country.* President Kennedy increased the defense readiness conditions ordered a **naval blockade** of ships heading toward Cuba.

Navy squadron VP (fixed-wing-patrol)-45, flew many missions during the **1962 Cuban Missile Crisis** and in 1976, I joined that squadron as we deployed to Iceland to hunt and track Soviet nuclear missile submarines at a time when the USSR was rapidly increasing it nuclear capabilities.

A retired Army officer recalled that 3 armored divisions *were enroute to Florida during the Cuban Missile Crisis and that the* **101ˢᵗ Airborne Division was on alert** *and soldiers were sleeping near aircraft during the crisis; their mission would be to* **parachute onto the missile sites in Cuba** *and disable them.*

Due to delays in passing messages during the Cuban Missile Crisis, the US and USSR implemented a **teletype *Hotline*** between Washington and Moscow to expedite communications in case of serious events. This hotline was first used by Washington to inform Moscow of the **assassination of President Kennedy** in November 1963.

Davy Crockett nuclear device (range 1.25 to 2.5 miles) *US Army*

Tactical Nuclear Operations In September 1954, the Soviet military conducted the ***"Snowball"* tactical exercise which included dropping a nuclear bomb and having various army forces maneuver around the radiated area.** The scale of this exercise surprised the US and caused a relook at nuclear plans which had been based solely on strategic air delivery of nuclear weapons. This shocked American planners because it **showed that**

the Soviets were planning to continue operations after a blast in radiated areas, were willing to accept massive casualties, and were developing army plans to utilize tactical nuclear weapons on land. Pentagon planners rapidly developed and deployed tactical nuclear weapons to enhance war plans.

The Soviets planned for both nuclear and conventional war capabilities with troops who could operate tactical nuclear weapons. They built up massive tank armies and nuclear capabilities aimed at breaking through the **Fulda Gap** to strike at the heart of West Germany.

The US Army concentrated on training soldiers who could operate on **atomic battlefields** and expedited development of new nuclear capabilities including the *Honest John and Little John* **missiles, artillery,** *Davy Crockett* **recoilless rifles, and land mines**. During these times, the Navy developed the nuclear-capable systems for tactical operations such as the *Regulus* and other missiles, ship/submarine/air delivered weapons including **nuclear depth bombs**.

   *According to a retired Army strategist:

"The Soviets were very practical in understanding that anyone's use of nukes, particularly their use in Western Europe, would create major physical impediments to their goal of conducting rapid penetrations and attacks in depth by their conventional ground forces. They even created special ground formations called Operational Maneuver Groups (OMGs) to go deep quickly so no one would get to use nukes."

Allied formations and the US Army *V Corps* with its large armored formations were deployed to counter the Soviet *8th Guards Army.* To counter overwhelming Soviet numbers advantage, the US developed the *Medium Atomic Demolition Munition* (land mine). In 1962 US Army troop strength in Europe peaked at 277,000.

   Cold War Nuclear Strategy and Agreements   In 1963, President Kennedy and Premier Khrushchev signed the ***Partial Nuclear Test Ban Treaty*** which banned atmospheric, oceanic, and outer space testing. This was the beginning of efforts between the Superpowers to improve communication, coordination, and to develop confidence building in the nuclear age.

President Lyndon Johnson recalled that "When I took office the air was somewhat less charged with blind anti-Communist sentiment. Americans felt a renewed self-confidence; which grew steadily over the years that followed...**Sputnik had given the Communists a tremendous psychological boost**, but by 1963 most Americans realized that the United States **was catching up and soon would pass the Soviets in space exploration**... Finally, the Soviet leaders had shown, by **their participation in the 'hotline' and in the Partial Test Ban Treaty,** that they were prepared to consider agreements that involved mutual benefits."[74]

Admiral James Stavridis, the former NATO Supreme Allied Commander for Global Operations, wrote that "The cold war was millions of well-trained troops on both sides facing one another across the **Fulda Gap** in Central Europe; it was **two huge battle fleets** playing cat and mouse from the High North and Arctic Circle to the bottom of the world off the coast of South America; it was two huge nuclear arsenals on a hair-trigger alert, **twenty thousand warheads** ready to utterly destroy the world."[75]

As the Superpower's nuclear arsenals grew, so did the risks from strategies such as **"preemptive first nuclear strike," second-strike capability, and "Mutually Assured Destruction (MAD)."**

In the 1960s, the US was perfecting **Multiple Independently Target Re-entry Vehicle (MIRV)** missiles and the Soviets were catching up. **John Newhouse, a former Assistant Director of the US Arms Control and Disarmament Agency,** wrote, "By 1967, the Soviets were well on the path to parity and their forces were less vulnerable. The superpowers were on the cusp between the first stage of their nuclear rivalry and the current stage...MIRV was a shining example of Washington's incurable tendency to exploit a technological lead. The "lead" invariably turns out to have been widely exaggerated. Sooner or later—usually sooner—the Soviet Union closes the gap and builds the same weapon. The balance of forces hasn't changed, but a weapon of greater versatility and destructive potential—a harder weapon to control—enters the

---

[74] Lyndon Baines Johnson, *The Vantage Point-Perspectives of the Presidency 1963-1969,* Holt, Rinehart and Winston, New York, 1971, p. 470

[75] Admiral James Stavridis, *Sea Power*, Penguin Press, New York, 2017, p. 82

superpower inventories...Whether it was politically wise or militarily possible to defend the Saigon government, and whether the costs of the commitment outweighed the benefits, are questions that historians continue to debate."[76]

From the 1960s through the '1980s, the US and USSR embarked on discussions and negotiated agreements to stabilize their nuclear stand-off and negotiate some standards in the arms race. Senior statesman W. Averill Harriman noted, "...But neither he (Robert Oppenheimer-key leader of the Manhattan Atom Bomb Project) nor the men who used the weapon, ever gave way completely to despair in the face of catastrophic power they held. In such resilience it is possible to find the thread of hope that also runs through our modern history, the faith that persistence and improvisation and innovation will bring us eventually to a durable center once again."[77]

Détente was a series of efforts by the Superpowers (and their allies) between 1969-1979 to increase dialogue and ease confrontations and tensions. *Détente* led to agreements including **SALT I, the Helsinki Accords, and SALT II** and ended with the 1979 Soviet invasion of Afghanistan. In 1975, President Ford represented the US and 35 European nations--including the Soviet Bloc countries--signed the **Helsinki Accords** to build confidence and reduce tensions within Europe.

According to Pat Buchanan, a speechwriter in the Nixon White House: "...But the **roots of détente can be traced to the earliest days of President Nixon.** Among the early signs that I noticed was the dialing back of the anticommunist content of US broadcasts to the Soviet Bloc, and the watering down of Captive Nations resolutions. These were annual declarations by the United States that the nations behind the Iron Curtain in Central and Eastern Europe, as well as Lithuania, Latvia, and Estonia, annexed by Stalin in 1940, were in reality captive countries, occupied and communized against their will. My sense was that Kissinger, who believed in a Metternichian concept of maintaining peace and security through

---

[76] John Newhouse, *War and Peace in the Nuclear Age,* New York; Alfred A. Knopf, Inc. 1988, pp. 202,203

[77] W. Averill Harriman in *The Twentieth Century-An Almanac,* Robert H. Ferrell, General Editor, New York; Bison Books Inc. 1985

a calculated balance of power, was diluting the moral content of the East-West struggle to secularize and de-ideologize the Cold War.[78]

The ***Strategic Arms Limitation Talks (SALT I) Agreement*** was signed in 1972, limiting ICBM and SLBM launchers and allowing each side to have 2 sites protected **Anti-Ballistic Missiles (ABM)**. The US protected **ICBM fields in South Dakota** and the **USSR protected Moscow**. Researcher Peter Almquist noted how some of the Soviet Union's key organizations operated, "During the SALT negotiations, for example, the Politburo reportedly met frequently to discuss United States proposals and Soviet responses."....."Those (doctrinal or policy decisions) that might have involved the defense industries include the decisions to enter the SALT process, the apparent conclusion by Brezhnev that the negative consequences of a nuclear war are likely to outweigh any gains, and the increasing emphasis on conventional forces in the 1970s. **Korolev and Sakharov, two of the most important military scientists, played roles in initiating the policy process on two other doctrinal decisions (rocketry and nuclear testing)**, and each was able to rally a number of other specialists to his cause in persuading the political leadership."[79]

[78] Pat Buchanan, *Nixon's White House Wars*, New York, Crown Publishing Group 2017, pp. 57-58

[79] Peter Almquist, *Red Forge, Soviet Military Industry Since 1965*, New York, Columbia University Press, 1990, pp. 16, 119-120

Chapter 9
Containment in Asia

After WWII, the French moved back into **Indochina** to reestablish colonial control (they threatened the US that they would not join NATO unless allowed back in their colonies) and the Americans based themselves in **Japan, the Philippines, and later Korea**). The US stationed hundreds of thousands of soldiers, sailors, and airmen throughout the Pacific to stabilize the vast region and thwart Communist political and military advances.

The prevailing Cold War concern was illustrated by the **Domino Theory** which held that countries would fall one-by one to Communism, and therefore, the West must make strong stands in Vietnam and other countries. **In 1954 President Eisenhower** stated "Finally, you have broader considerations that might follow what you would call **the "falling domino" principle.** You have a row of dominoes set up, you knock over the first one, and what will happen to the last one is the certainty that it will go over very quickly. So you could have a beginning of a disintegration that would have the most profound influences."[80]

To contain communism, eight nations signed the Manila Pact in 1954 to create the **South East Asian Treaty Organization (SEATO).** The only South East Asian countries in SEATO were Thailand and the Philippines; the others were Australia, New Zealand, Pakistan, United Kingdom, France, and the United States. SEATO lasted until 1977.

Many senior Filipino leaders had sided with the Japanese during WWII and had been seeking independence from the US for decades. Stanley Kornow reported from Asia for many years

---

[80] *"The Quotable Quotes of Dwight D. Eisenhower,"* National Park Service. December 5, 2013

starting in 1959 and observed, "If MacArthur sculpted the political shape of the **postwar Philippines**, other Americans pressed the archipelago into the US military and economic fold...But aside from a few ultranationalists, Filipinos generally welcomed the so-called special relationship as proof of America's concern for their welfare. The relationship was periodically roiled during the postwar years by controversies—prime among them the status of Clark airfield and the Subic navy yard, America's largest overseas bases. Many Filipinos have maintained that the bases violate their sovereignty as well as **imperil their security by making them a potential target in case of war between the superpowers.**"[81]

Sukarno, the leading Indonesian nationalist, had collaborated with the Japanese during WWII, fought the Dutch for independence after the war, and was imprisoned by them. In 1948 the **Indonesia Communist Party (PKI)** attempted a rebellion which was put down. Sukarno was named President in 1949, led anti-imperialist policies, and accepted Soviet aid. He helped organize and hosted the **1955 *Bandung Conference*** of 29 African and Asian countries and promoted *Newly Emerging Forces (NEFOS).*[82]

Sukarno **nationalized Dutch companies** in 1957 and fought Dutch, British, and American interests. He withdrew Indonesia from the United Nations in 1965 and promoted an anti-imperialist alliance of Asian Communist nations based on a "Beijing-Jakarta" axis. Sukarno tried to balance various Indonesian forces including the military, Islamists, nationalists, and the PKI. After a failed coup attempt by communist-leaning officers in 1965 and the subsequent killing of hundreds of thousands of communists and ethnic Chinese, General Suharto replaced Sukarno in 1966.

During the ***Malayan Emergency*** 1948-1960, British Commonwealth forces successfully suppressed a communist insurgency fueled by ethnic Chinese factions. Malaya was a completely different conflict on a tiny scale compared to the long Vietnam wars; yet Malaya provided a successful precedent which

---

[81] Stanley Kornow, *In Our Image; America's Empire in the Philippines*, Ballantine Books-Random House, New York 1989. P. 330

[82] H.R. Cowie, *Australia and Asia. A changing Relationship*, 1993, p.18

emboldened American planners to take-on the massive North Vietnamese Army and Viet Cong guerrilla threats in South Vietnam.

1st Air Cavalry (Airmobile) *US Army*

Southeast Asia The ***Viet Minh*** soundly defeated the French at the siege of **Dien Bien Phu in 1954** and the United States increased its involvement in Vietnam. In the early '60s, President Kennedy sent Army Special Forces ***"A Teams"* to Vietnam** to strengthen South Vietnam's fight against Communism and publicly announced our previous covert support for Laos. For an overview of Vietnam, see the new Ken Burns PBS film *"The Vietnam War."* [83]

Former Army OV-1 ***Mohawk* airman Robert Curry** summed-up his views of the Vietnam experience and his participation in the secret war in Laos:

*"Betrayal is seldom a term that invokes a sense of political impartiality, but then, the **Vietnam era betrayed all normal political definition and predictability.** No matter what side of the political spectrum, the sense of betrayal was rampant... Americans, always ready to spill the blood of their sons and daughters to help deliver freedom in some far-flung corner*

---

[83] *The Vietnam War,* film by Ken Burns and Lynn Novick, PBS 2017

*of the world, had their morals as a nation questioned. The military could no longer trust Washington, who showed no clear direction, but daily imposed new rules which cost thousands of lives. A Washington who tried to mandate which regimes would rule. That noble goal was never decided in the ballot box, only on the battlefield. **When Washington grew tired and confused, the lofty goals of freedom and self-determination turned to political survival.***

In 1969, an eighteen year-old, stubborn in his belief that his duty was to follow the call of a nation, went to war. I believed in mom, apple pie, and that our cause was always just, but more than anything, I wanted to fly...

*These fierce Hmong warriors kept **one hundred thousand of North Vietnam's finest troops tied up in Laos**. These battle-seasoned troops would have been sent to the battles waging in South Vietnam, causing additional untold death and destruction upon the Americans serving there."*[84]

Laos Secret War To counter rapidly growing North Vietnamese Army and **Pathet Lao** (local Communist) aggression in Laos and the *Ho Chi Minh Trail* area, in 1961 President Kennedy directed the CIA to train thousands of volunteers into **Special Guerrilla Units (SGU)** led by General Vang Pao. In 1962, covert American advisors came out in the open as uniformed **White Star Mobile Training Teams.**

*According to Yang Chee, former President of the *Lao-Hmong American Coalition*:

*"**The Hmong SGU provided...soldiers, pilots, Forward Air Controllers & Guides, Backseaters, Intelligence Officers, Translators/Interpreters, Special Operations Team, Commandos, Airborne troopers, nurses, and medics**. They faithfully provided safeguard for U.S. personnel, guarded USAF radar installations, and gathered critical intelligence about enemy operations and their positions. They served as vital communications links for American armed Forces engaging in strategic bombing missions. They also undertook dangerous*

---

[84] Robert Curry, *Whispering Death; Our Journey With the Hmong in the Secret War for Laos*, iUniverse, Inc Lincoln NE 2004, pp.xix, xxi

*tasks for conducting Search and Rescue missions to save the lives of many downed American pilots...**more than half of the courageous Hmong pilots were killed in action**....As a result of the 'Secret War', out of an ethnic population of about 300,000 **over 35,000 Hmong fighters lost their lives for the cause of freedom.***"* [85]

*Lao-mong Special Guerrilla Unit Veterans (the officer on the right was held as a **POW for 19 years**) DCS photo*

Former Ambassador to Laos G. McMurtrie Godley stated, "We used the Hmong. The rationale...was that they tied down three first-rate North Vietnamese divisions that otherwise would have been used against our men in South Vietnam. It was a dirty business." [86]

President Johnson used the **1964 *Gulf of Tonkin Incident*** to justify sending more troops to Vietnam and to prove his toughness against Communism after being goaded by Senator Barry Goldwater and conservatives. American public opinion supported his stance. **In early 1965 Marines landed near Danang and the 1st Air Cavalry (Airmobile) entered Vietnam** to start the rapid build-up of troops which peaked at about 550,000 troops in 1968—the year LBJ decided not to run for re-election.

In March 1965, Assistant Secretary John McNaughton laid out **stark Vietnam policy realities** in his memorandum to Secretary

---

[85] Yang Chee, *History of the Lao-Hmong Special Guerrilla Units (SGU) Veterans,* Lao-Hmong American Coalition, Westminster, CO 2005

[86] Roger Warner, *Back Fire: The CIA's Secret War in Laos and Its Link to the War in Vietnam,* New York, Simon & Schuster 1995 p. 362

of Defense Robert McNamara: *"Proposed Course of Action re: Vietnam; Annex-Plan of Action for South Vietnam:*

1. US aims: 70% --To avoid a humiliating US defeat (to our reputation as a guarantor). 20%--To keep SVN (South Vietnam and then adjacent) territory from Chinese hands. 10%--To permit the people of SVN to enjoy a better, freer way of life.

2. *The situation*: **The situation in general is bad and deteriorating. The VC have the initiative.** Defeatism is gaining among the rural population, somewhat in the cities, and even among the soldiers--especially those with relatives in rural areas. The Hop Tac area around Saigon is making little progress; the Delta stays bad; the country has been severed in the north. GVN control is shrinking to enclaves, some burdened with refugees. In Saigon we have a remission: Quat is giving hope on the civilian side, the Buddhists have calmed, and the split generals are in uneasy equilibrium."[87]

1968 Camp Eagle outside of Phu Bai (South of Hue) SGT Ralph Timmons (3rd from right) LRRP team leader and oldest member at 24; at least 3 of the team were 18 or 19 *Ralph Timmons photo*

---

[87] Draft Memorandum from McNaughton to Robert McNamara, *"Proposed Course of Action re: Vietnam"* 24 March 1965; *The Pentagon Papers*, Gravel Edition, Volume 3, pp. 694-702

*101ˢᵗ Airborne Long Range Reconnaissance Patrol (LRRP) Team Leader Ralph Timmons recalls his service:

*If you are like me growing up, you probably **knew a good number of veterans and were as in awe of them as I was. I think that a big part of my motivation was to emulate them**. The other singular thing that spoke to our generation was **John Kennedy's call "Don't ask what your country can do for you, ask what you can do for your country." Those two things set me on the course I took, and even with prior knowledge I'd do it over again.***

*In early **January 1962** having recently completed Marine boot camp, infantry training and attained my 18ᵗʰ birthday I found myself on a troop transport on my way to 13 months on Okinawa. One of the highlights of that year occurred during the summer when my company was selected to be trained in jungle warfare and in turn act as aggressors during the training of the rest of the battalion's companies. **The trainers were two senior NCOs whom the Marine Corps had sent to Malaya where the Brits were engaged in a guerilla war with communist insurgents**. The Marine Corps obviously sensed that might be of use in the future.*

***By 1965 the Marines were involved in Vietnam and extended the enlistments by four months for all Marines** in order to enlist and train enough Marines to meet their new manpower commitments. I immediately volunteered for duty in Vietnam. In early **January 1966** I was once again on my way to Okinawa and an LST headed for Da Nang, Vietnam. For the next 6 months I was a radio technician assigned to a detached **Amphibian Tractor (AmTrac) platoon near Hue**. By September I was on my way back to the states enrolled in college.*

It did not take me long among the draft dodgers at college to decide I much preferred a military life. I thought the Army offered me more options than periodic trips to Okinawa so I enlisted. At the time I had a brother serving in the 173ʳᵈ Airborne Brigade in Vietnam. I reasoned that I would not be sent back to Vietnam, but I would go to jump school and avoid having to listen to his ribbing. **Big miscalculation! I finished jump school and received orders to Vietnam arriving on December 7, 1967.**

The 101ˢᵗ Airborne Division *was arriving in country and all personnel in the replacement center that were airborne qualified were flagged from their assignments and sent to fill out their vacancies. I wound up at their in-country orientation for a week of learning--much that I already knew. Then about half way through the week we received a* **recruiting pitch from some men in tiger fatigues challenging us to volunteer for the LURP Company**. *I had already decided that I wouldn't be able to face any future grandchildren if I spent the war in an air-conditioned van fixing radios. Anyway, I figured I had all of that jungle training and it seemed a shame to waste it.* **So I volunteered and was selected.**

The Lurp Company was in the process of integrating the personnel who came with the Division, those Lurps that had been assigned to the Brigade of the 101ˢᵗ that had been sent to Vietnam many months before, and the few of us who had been sent to the 101ˢᵗ as replacements. The Company was sent to **Song Be about 50 miles Northwest of Saigon to help defend a Special Forces detachment and an airfield in a Michelin Rubber Plantation**. *We arrived just ahead of the North Vietnamese hordes bent on taking over the South. What fun!*

Shortly after Tet the company moved to the Hue/Phu Bai area to establish Camp Eagle, the home of the Screaming Eagles. It was there that I met a recent graduate of the **MACV Recondo School**. *He was the Honor Graduate of his class. He had a neat Special Forces knife with an engraved blade and more importantly, had been promoted to Sergeant by the Division Commander. I already had a couple of missions under my belt so without much thought I volunteered.*

From 1966-1968, the **Recondo School at Nha Trang** *(started by MACV General Westmoreland) was operated by* **5ᵗʰ Special Forces Group Ranger instructors** *to train American and Allied soldiers in* **Long-Range Reconnaissance Patrolling** *techniques. The* **3-week long** *Recondo course included practice patrolling,* *team member responsibilities, radio procedures, weapons, navigation, rappelling, escape-and-evasion ambush, first aid, and **ended with a combat patrol. The MACV Recondo course has a failure rate of 50 percent.***

*The primary function of the school was to turn out well- qualified and competent Team Leaders. The 101st Airborne Division sent people not only from the LRP company, but also some of the **line unit's quick reaction forces. These "Blue Teams" were usually platoon size and had missions like recovering crews and equipment from crash sites and Lurp teams in contact.** They were **often used as "bait" to go in and fix an enemy** until a larger unit could be inserted to develop the situation.*

*My reason for volunteering for the unit in the first place was that I felt my prior training and experience would be an asset to the unit and I suppose **I wanted to test myself**. I was also attracted to the school because it would give me a **chance earn a stripe** if I could become the honor graduate of my class. At any rate, I went to the school in mid-May, 1968.*

*My class started with at least **50 people and was composed of personnel from Army units and three teams from the Marine Corps, The Republic of Korea and Thailand. We graduated 23.** All of these individuals were highly motivated and competitive. The training was tough and at times almost brutal. There is an adage that "they can make you wish you were dead, but they can't kill you." I embraced the game and I accomplished what I sat out to do.*

*I considered myself fortunate to have successfully completed the course, let alone **graduate at the top of the class, which I did.** As a result, I got the promotion and my own team when I returned to the Division. More importantly, the skills, competence and confidence the school instilled in not only myself but in all who completed the course undoubtedly contributed to success of the units they represented. It was one of the better moments and accomplishments of my military career and is **one of the reasons I was fortunate to not lose anyone.***

*Our LRRP table of organization called for 6-man teams, but I never took out more than a **5-man team because of personnel shortages**. Often, I had to take one or more personnel from other teams to conduct a patrol. Team leaders could reject personnel for any reason at any time. Personal feelings and gut instincts played a significant part of those decisions, but were essential to the confidence and competence of the team.*

*We were part of F Company, 58th Infantry,101st Airborne Division. It was re-designated shortly after I left, to L Company, 75th Rangers, 101st ABN DIV. All Division LRP units were re-designated at the same time. We are all considered legacy units of the currently serving **75th Ranger Regiment** whose lineage traces back to **Merrill's Marauders.** F Company was activated as such from January 1968 to February 1969. I believe that L Company was active until the 101st was returned to CONUS in 1973.*

*An excerpt from "6 Silent Men Part Two" tells about one patrol I still remember: "He (Sgt Timmons) unsealed his ration package and had taken a couple of bites when he sensed a presence and had the spooky feeling that someone was watching him. He looked up and there it was, **a very big and black leopard**. The leopard stepped around the man next to Timmons and moved closer. It was amazing how silently the big cat could move—and it was amazing how close it was...It seemed more interested in Timmons than in what Timmons was eating. The tip of its tail twitching, the big cat sniffed Timmon's foot and then his leg, then it snorted softly, shook his head and walked past the rest of the team members showing little interest in them. As suddenly and silently as it had come, it was gone.*

*Moments later, the team heard a noise on the trail. Everyone froze and watched intently as **a squad of eight NVA soldiers** with SKS rifles slung on their backs and shovels in their hands came down the trail past them. The NVA were very relaxed and nonchalant, talking amongst themselves and not paying much attention to their surroundings...word was whispered through the team that the NVA had entered an encampment further down the trail—an* *encampment the team had somehow missed earlier. **Very slowly—very, very slowly and carefully, the team edged a little closer. NVA could be seen stacking ammunition and crates big enough to contain 122mm rockets.***

***The team eased away, stepping very cautiously, ready for all hell to break loose**...McKinnon called in the sighting and soon word was passed back that the team was to get back to the LZ as quickly as possible for extraction...**They moved back through the complex of fighting positions and across the maze of trails to the LZ**...They moved to the edge of the LZ and set up a tight perimeter...The extraction ship came in fast and low, the door gunners firing up the woodline on either side with their M60s. The team broke cover, then dashed for the bird and clambered aboard, and the bird nosed out, banked to the left and picked up airspeed.*

*Once on the ground back at Camp Eagle, the team was rushed into the debriefing tent...Almost before the debriefing was over, word came back that an airstrike had gone into the area and **two large secondary explosions** had been triggered by the bombing. This pleased the Lurps."*[88]

*When a team is surrounded and can't get to a drop zone, these **110-foot ropes were anchored to the floor of a Huey and are dropped through the trees** where team members can tie in and be lifted up and out. Only drawback is it takes two lifts to extract a 5 or 6-man team. Another problem is the people on the ropes must hold tight to each other otherwise they may begin to swing and destabilize the aircraft.*

*One time we were trying to get to an extraction point, we had to **climb-out via a 30-foot rope ladder** because of the steep hillside. We had been inserted on a ridge line and as soon as we were on the ground, the **VC began to search for us with dogs** and firing as they began moving toward us.*

---

[88] Kenn Miller, *Six Silent Men Book Two*, New York, Mass Market Paperback Ivy Books 1997 pp. 81-83

Lurps Practicing McGuire Rig extractions *Ralph Timmons photo*

***Ralph Timmons** served 5 years in the United States Marine Corps from 1961 to 1966 and then 17 years in the United States Army retiring in August 1984. He served 18 months in Vietnam including 6 months in the US Marine Corps as an infantryman and as a ground radio communications repairman and 12 months with the US Army. During his Army career he served as an infantryman including **Infantry Operations and Intelligence (Long Range Reconnaissance),** Recruiting Station Commander, Platoon Sergeant Mechanized Infantry, US Army Reserve Augmentee Program (G-3) and **Infantry Company First Sergeant**. Ralph was commissioned a First Lieutenant (dual status) in the US Army Reserve and his decorations include the Combat Infantry Badge, the Marine Corps Combat Action Ribbon, the US Army Parachute Badge, the MACV *Recondo* Patch and the US Army Recruiter Badge (three gold stars). He was awarded the **Bronze Star Medal w/V Device**, the Meritorious Service Medal (two Oak Leaf Clusters), the Vietnam Service Medal, the Vietnam Gallantry Cross with Palm, Vietnam Campaign Medal with 7 Campaign Stars, and the Presidential Unit Citation (Navy and Army).

After retiring from the military, Ralph completed a 20-year career in Federal Civil Service as a Program and Management Analyst retiring as a GS-14. During his career he worked for the Veterans Administration, the General Accounting Office, the Federal Aviation Administration, and the Transportation Security Administration. Ralph holds a Bachelor of Arts degree and is a Life member of the **75ᵗʰ Ranger Regiment Association**, the American Legion, and the Veterans of Foreign Wars.

1968 Bob Evans at *LZ Sharon* (Quang Tri)

*Former Huey pilot Bob Evans remembers Vietnam:

*Interesting that your draft brought back memories of **April 19, 1968 when the 1ˢᵗ Cav (Airmobile) sent up a gaggle of nearly 100 birds (Huey helicopters) to make the initial assault into the A Shau Valley.** Our company (Bravo, 229th Avn Bn.) was the lead that day. The cloud cover was such that we had to **climb (staggered trail formation) to nearly 13,000 feet. We (UH1H "Hueys") had a service ceiling of 14,000 feet;** however, we were loaded with fully combat ready troops, so the **controls were a bit mushy at 13,000 feet,** and we were **pulling nearly 45 pounds of torque with our max set at 50.** Many of us lost our cherries that day, my right-seat guy **took a round through his foot and*** *on landing, we found our tail boom well laced with a dozen neat holes.*

By April 22, the assault teams had moved into the valley proper and set-up shop on the A Shau airstrip. At around 1630 on April 23, the Battalion Commander called for a bird to be stationed at his TOC (Tactical Operations Center) over night. **One of the most senior pilots and I raised our hands to take one of the B229 birds in. It should be noted that the A Shau Valley was zero/zero (no visibility with fog) that evening;** *however, the Air Force had brought in a portable GCA unit (Ground Controlled Approach), and both the GCA operator and the Battalion Commander wanted to make sure it was operational.*

We lifted off from LZ Sharon at around 18:00. At the LZ, we had a 500-foot ceiling, so we were able to lift off VFR (Visual Flight Rules); however, we were soon enveloped and were IFR (Instrument Flight Rules). **This was my first time flying IFR without wearing a hood and having an instructor tapping (beating on) my helmet with a metal ruler.** *The excellent training did come in very handy that evening. The GCA operator painted us after a couple of acquisition turns and we were on* **glideslope flying between two mountains into a very narrow valley.**

We broke out at no more than 10 feet at a hover and set the bird down. We tied down the main rotor, opened cans of C Rations, found a couple cans of Carlings, broke out our poncho liners and bedded down in the Bell Hotel...Mission accomplished.

Bob Evans an Army "brat," was in his senior year at the University of New Mexico when he and his fraternity roommate, also an Army "brat" **decided to sign up for the Army Warrant Office Flight Program, knowing full-well the path would lead to Vietnam.** After 14 months of training, it was off to Vietnam and the **First Air Cavalry Division. *Bob received the Silver Star for July 1968 troop extraction from the base of Hill 881 near Khe Sanh under enemy fire.

Near the end of tour one **in December 1968, he received a direct commission to Second Lieutenant**, returned to CONUS and

Artillery Basic Course. After the Basic Course, Bob spent a year at Fort Hood Texas as a Battery Executive Officer, **and then off to Vietnam for tour two**. He mustered out of the Army at the rank of Captain in 1971. He used the **GI Bill** to finish his undergraduate degree and his **PhD in Psychology. He taught at the University of New Mexico and the University of Arkansas before joining the Nuclear Utility business**. He retired from the Nuclear Energy Institute in 2004, joined 3M Company as the National Market Director that same year and retired from 3M in 2015.

1967: Mixed Citizen Support for Vietnam According to the *New York Times* "In a **(1967)** Gallup poll, **25 % of Americans from both parties supported using nuclear weapons against the North Vietnamese**. Meanwhile a Harris Poll found growing support for escalation; **45% backed a more aggressive American approach** to the war, while 41% supported de-escalation."[89]

President Johnson and his Department of Defense needed more troops to rapidly build-up forces in Vietnam and Congress passed the **Military Selective Service Act of 1967** which expanded the draft to ages **18-35** and **ended deferments for college beyond 4-year degrees.**

*Our neighbor was in law school at this time and he told us that "**he had gotten caught-up in LBJ's cleaning-out the law schools."** He enlisted, went through Army infantry officer training, and was immediately sent to the Vietnam Delta region where he was severely wounded.*

During 1967-68 President Johnson built-up forces in Vietnam to over 500,000 troops (peaking at **549,500 in 1969 under President Nixon**). These forces required massive long-term logistic supply operations and Malcolm McLean pioneered **shipping containers** and purpose-built ships which carried supplies to the troops.[90]

The Army had highly-trained elite units and specialists (*101st Airborne, 173rd Airborne, 1st Air Cavalry*, etc.), however, to meet

---

[89] *The New York Times*, May 1967
[90] *Containers; 50 Things That Made the Modern Economy*, BBC, http://www.bbc.co.uk/programmes/b08jbd20

demands to build-up in-country troop levels rapidly, draftees were trained quickly to get them into the fight in Vietnam. **Draftees had a 2-year commitment with 13 months in country and then rotated back to the US.**

After 5 soldiers were killed in 1969 when a New Hampshire National Guard truck was blown-up by a road mine, the Department of Defense stopped deploying units together and sent individual soldiers to fill-in unit gaps—hence the *"new guy"* syndrome where a new soldier would show-up and no one wanted to get to him as the *new guy* casualty rates were so high.

The Army was desperate for officers and scraped the bottom of barrel at times. LT William Calley, *one of many people pushed by senior officers for body counts and results,* was convicted for the March 1968 My Lai massacre. He had been a Florida junior college drop-out and held several jobs including being a conductor on a railroad.

DD-786 getting new gun barrels in Danang 1972

The Navy maintained a very high ops-tempo constantly deploying many ships and personnel to the Vietnam theater and the South China Sea for airstrikes, naval gunfire support (NGFS, and *"Brown Water"* river patrol duties. **The Navy and the Coast Guard** deployed ships for naval gunfire support and *Operation Market Time* missions around Vietnam to cut-off supplies to communist forces. P5s, P-2s, and P-3s flew many patrols in support of *Market Time.*

1971 Ltjg Cowan and Pacific Fleet
Commander Admiral J.S. McCain Jr. *USCG*

*Coast Guard Captain Michael Cowan's career ranged from service in Southeast Asia through the end of the Cold War:

When I served aboard USCGC Winnebago (a Lake Class Cutter), the USS Pueblo was moored outboard us in Yokosuka the last week of 1967 just before they were captured. We were on the pier head after moving the USS Reeves aft - our CO was a Mustang (former enlisted) O6 sent to clean-up a mess and outranked the larger ship.

Winnebago later deployed to Southeast Asia for **Operation Market Time**. *We provided naval gunfire support and supplies to units in-country and closer to shore in Vietnam. Ammunition and fuel came via underway replenishment from supply ships passing through the patrol area every few days. On one relief break in Subic Bay Philippines, I saw a Navy Warrant Officer W4 with his khaki "50 mission" combo cap and appropriate-sized cigar get out of his personal Government Vehicle marked:*

COMASWFORPACSUPREPWESPAC across both doors. Priceless!

As Key West Group Commander (1980-1982), I attended the CJTF 115 flag brief once per week by invitation. They were closely watching regional Soviet activities as I'm sure the other side was watching ours. We knew the TU-95 Bear triangle flight schedule (Russia, Angola, Cuba) to the minute. The Aerostat "Fat Albert" was always watching the Florida straits and communications then – and still is.

***Captain Cowan grew up in Oregon, graduated from the US Coast Guard Academy in 1967, and specialized in Shore Operations and Search and Rescue (SAR). He served as Weapons Officer on the High Endurance Cutter *USCGC Winnebago* deployed to Vietnam and then worked in recruit training at TRASUPCEN Alameda. Captain Cowan went to the Naval Postgraduate School and received an MS in Operations Research, followed by staff tours developing computer-based SAR planning tools. He was **Key West Group Commander during the 1980 Mariel (Cuba) Boatlift** and the Florida interdiction resources buildup before staff assignments at CGD5 and Coast Guard Headquarters (CGHQ). Captain Cowan was **Galveston Group Commander** during the T/S Mega Borg fire, fisheries enforcement campaigns, and the Trinity River floods. His final assignment was SAR Program Director at CGHQ. After retiring from the Coast Guard, he worked 14 years as a test engineer and training expert for BAE Systems on **NOAA/NASA/USAF weather satellite programs** and then 2 years as an Operations Research Analyst for Alion on **U.S Army Staff electronics warfare alternatives analysis**.

In 1967-68, *VO-67* (Observation Squadron 67) flew dangerous electronic **Trail Road Interdiction Missions (TRIM)** over the Ho Chi Minh Trail in OP-2E *Neptunes;* **in this one squadron 20 crewmen perished on 3 aircraft.**

One day, a mild-mannered government attorney (and Navy Intel Reserve Captain) I worked with, mentioned that he had flown as an NFO on P-2 missions over the Ho Chi Minh Trail—he must have been with VO-67; RIP Dan Hurley and all your brave squadron mates.

OP-2E (callsign *"Mud River"*) over Vietnam *by Dusty Reynolds USN (VO-67), Navy Naval Aviation News* July 1981 p.33

Chuck Morris in *poopie suit* on a cold wintry day at Misawa
Chuck Morris photo

*P-2 Radio Operator Chuck Morris recalls operating from Misawa and Iwakuni, Japan; Sangley Point and Cubi Point Philippines; Saigon and Cam Ranh Bay Vietnam:

*During our 1966 - 1967 deployment to Misawa Air Base, Northern Japan, I did not like wearing the **orange survival "poopie suits"** which we needed as we flew up towards Arctic waters in the* north and west Pacific. **The flying was lonely, miserable, cold with bumpy air (always airsick)** and the flights were over large expanses of the Northwest Pacific Ocean, **with bad wind currents, and threats from Korea and Russia.**

On the **night of December 3, 1966 we were on short final to Tan Son Nhut Airbase** Vietnam and almost on the runway, when the VC attacked. US Air Force historians have a great record of this. We waved off when the tower said we were under attack, orbited, and then went **15 miles over to Bien Hoa Air Base** to wait it out and refuel to come back much later in the following day.

We were **flying out of Cam Ranh Bay** and during our patrols along the coast of Vietnam, we worked with the surface craft, and one day we traded rides; I got a ride on a PCF, Swift Boat out of **Nha Trang**, One night, we were on SE Asia patrol, way down south at the southern tip of Vietnam and on the intercom, Radar was talking about a large target on the radar screen and we did not get any info on who that would be, so we did a run in on it, lit off the searchlight, and alas, it was one of our very own aircraft carriers, Constellation or Kitty Hawk, I don't remember. The comment on the intercom was that anyone on outside watch on the ship was probably to go inside and get relieved because **their night vision was probably wrecked from that searchlight.**

I got zapped one time by St Elmo's fire while we were in the clouds out over the South China Sea, I was having a chance to sit up front in the bow observer station, headset on, it was cloudy, and I started hearing this clicking and static on my headset, so, I grabbed them to take them off because I had a feeling what was to come, sure enough, I got zapped, I crawled down the tunnel as fast as I could, I hit the floor hatch to crawl up out of there into the flight deck, just my luck, somebody was taking a nap right on top of that hatch, I still got out, with wide eyes and lots of stories.

As a P-2 Radio Operator (VP-17) in the mid - late 1960's in Southeast Asia patrols, we received boxes of C-rations. The *canned foods, some of which could be heated, I put those up **on top of the ARC-27 UHF radio, it was a perfect surface to hold the cans and heat them.** I actually hate lima beans, but, the **C-rats ham & lima beans were good when warmed up by the UHF radio.***

*...Another story when the coffee was still hot and being sent aft, over the wing beam. Someone was napping next to the radio operator on the floor, and **the coffee pot slid over the wing beam** and landed and dumped hot coffee on the guy laying there.*

P-2 and R-3350 on Cubi Point ramp near *USS Enterprise* (CVN-65) *Chuck Morris photo*

*We worked temporarily out of NAS Cubi Point in the Philippines while Sangley Point was undergoing runway repairs. I had been through a few engine failures before, but the one that really got me was when we were at takeoff power out of Cubi Point and the **R-3350 engine blew up and scared the daylights out of me.** We were co-located on the same ramp alongside USS Enterprise (CVN-65).*

***AT1 Chuck Morris enlisted in US Navy in **September 1963**, went through aviation training in Tennessee, then San Diego, then to survival training out of San Diego. July 1965 to the Fleet at NAS Whidbey Island, **Patrol Squadron 17 from 1965-68**, and immediately to MCAS Iwakuni, Japan, at a **rear base for operations in Vietnam**. He did **3 deployments to SE Asia**; on the **last 2 deployments he was flight crew tech and radio operator.** In 1968 I went back home and decided not stay in the active duty Navy, so I spent the next year in **VP-42 at Whidbey Island**, not on flight duties any more, and was discharged from the USN in August 1969. Chuck retired in 2005 from the telecommunications industry as a equipment technician on a wide variety of systems and telecom gear. He lives in Clackamas, Oregon, 15 miles southeast of Portland, Oregon.

ATN2 Chuck Morris and blown R-3350 at Cubi Point *Chuck Morris photo*

*Commander (Ret.) Steve Thiel Remembers volunteering for Vietnam on *PBRs*.

*I hadn't realized what a dumb thing I had done volunteering for PBRs (Patrol Boat Riverine) until February of '68 when we were on the Perfume River underway to the **City of Hue** (northern part of South Vietnam) and getting dumped on in an NVA ambush. I realized I had perhaps made a very very big mistake. I had been married for four months, paid for a lifetime subscription to Gourmet Magazine, and quit smoking and I think it was the **B-40s (rocket propelled grenades) and .50 Cal incoming** that convinced me of the error of my decision. We cleared the kill zone* *and continued up river.* **I bummed a cigarette from my boat captain, reasoned that my mother would get my magazine subscriptions for 10 years, and my bride would receive $15 grand from my SGLI (insurance).**

MkII PBR (Patrol Boat Riverine, crew 4, speed 29 kts) *US Army Center of Military History*

In 1966 I was a Ltjg, the personnel officer at Sangley Point Naval Station, and had one year of active duty left in the Navy. I was sitting at my desk on a hot, muggy Philippine afternoon when Commander Lausch came to my desk in the Personnel office with the latest copy of All Hands and said "Here is a great job for a young Naval Officer." It was an article on the new boats in the Navy: the **PBRs and Swifts.** *Later that afternoon, we met at the O Club for happy hour and he again told me how really neat one of these boats would be. All I had to do was to volunteer to extend my active duty service in the Navy if assigned to one of these new class of boats. After several lumpias, San Miguels, and much talk how great it would be going to Vietnam, I decided I would volunteer.*

Swift boat (PCF Patrol Coast Fast, crew 6, speed 21 kts) *Chuck Morris photo*

*The next day I mailed off a letter requesting assignment to either PBRs or Swifts, but my detailer wrote back saying I was not qualified for this duty because I was not a qualified underway OOD (ship Officer of the Deck). My commanding officer, Captain James M. (Crash) Johnson was not happy with my detailer's reply. At about the same time the Commanding Officer of the USCG Nettle (WAK 109), had asked CAPT Johnson if he could spare an officer to go aboard the Nettle for a deployment to Vietnam/ Thailand. The Old Man replied that he could and would. I was cut orders to the Nettle and qualified as a fleet OOD. The **Egypt-Israel Seven Day War (1967)** was fought while we were at sea and we didn't even hear about it; very limited comm aboard so we did not get news broadcasts.*

*RADM Kossler endorsed my letter and had his deputy, hand-carry my letter to BuPer and not many days later I got a postcard form my Detailer congratulating me on my persistence, and telling me I would be receiving orders as a Patrol Officer aboard PBRs in Vietnam. My orders to me to Vietnam via **San Diego for Vietnam Indoc, SERE, language school, and then to Naval Station Vallejo for 6 weeks of Navy Inshore Off Coast Training (NIOCT)**. It was a great school; we were well-trained and indoctrinated by* *a Navy LT who was in the first group of Navy SEALs. He was as tough as nails, an ex-Boatswain Mate whose first tour of shore duty was to Luzon Philippines in 1943.*

*At NIOCT we learned that **our mission in Vietnam was interdiction of the waterways, population control, and psychological operations**. Classes included emergency repairs to boat engines and water jets. We had to be able to diagnose and make the repairs in total darkness and also were timed. We learned weapons: .50 Cal machine gun, M60, M16, M1, .45 Cal pistol, and Mk 49 grenade launcher. I still can field-strip and time a .50 Cal machine gun in total darkness. This training paid off in Nam since most of us ended up doing these repairs in combat and many times in darkness.*

*The PBR was a versatile boat with a fiberglass hull and waterjet drive which enabled it to operate in shallow, weed-choked rivers. **It drew only two feet of water fully loaded. The drives could be pivoted to reverse direction, turn the boat in its own length, or come to a stop from full speed in a few boat lengths.** The PBR was manufactured in two versions, the first with 31-foot length and 10-foot, 7-inch beam. The Mark II version 32 feet (9.8 m) long and one-foot wider beam, had improved drives to reduce fouling, and aluminum gunwales to resist wear.*

*After graduation and a first-class ass-chewing by the CO of NICOT, CAPT Lemon, we were bused to Travis AFB and flown to the Clark AFB then bussed to NAS Cubi Point for one week of **Jungle Environmental Survival Training (JEST)**. It was great fun; the Igorot instructors were fantastic and made the week in jungle interesting, educational and fun. After a week of fun in the jungle it was off to Nam.*

*We arrived just in time for the **1968 Tet Offensive**. Prior to boarding the plane, we were told to get rid of everything we could not run with, no civies and no dress uniforms (camies only). It was a short flight to Saigon's **Tan Son Nhut Airport**. We ran from the plane into the terminal which had been hit the night before,* *then boarded a bus and were taken to the **Annapolis Hotel** (any resemblance between the Annapolis and a hotel was purely coincidental)! We slept on cots under the stars inside the hotel (the roof had been opened by mortars prior to our arrival). We walked a block to the chow hall, hugging the bulkheads, and looking for sand bags while listening to sporadic gun fire.*

*Somewhere along the way back we found a bar selling Ba Muy Ba, Vietnam's only beer which is very good, but not as good as San Mig. The next day we were bused to NSA Saigon for further transportation to our boat section. Since my boat section had not been commissioned, LT Santi who was to be the OinC of the section I was ordered to, another LT, and I were sent to **CTF Clearwater which was aboard the Mobile Support Barge One (MSB 1)**. I had no idea that I had been assigned to the CTF until all Navy personal records were put on microfische and the paper was sent to us. Not only was I assigned to the CTF, but my billet was **Psychological Operations Officer which explains why I was sent to PsyOps at the 3rd Marines in Da Nang after Tet was over.***

We flew to Da Nang to report to the Swift Boat Operations for further transportation to the MSB 1. The airport was under constant shelling and no one there could or would tell us how to get the Naval Support Activity (NAVSUPACT) Da Nang. So, we grabbed our duffel bags, left the terminal, and went into the parking lot with the hopes of catching a ride. A person whom we thought was a Navy Commander had just pulled up in a jeep so we saluted him and asked him if he could give us a ride. He promptly informed he was an Air Force Lt Col and was too busy to be a taxi driver or tell us where Naval Supply Activity Da Nang was located or how to get there.

The two Naval Academy grads that I was there with were pondering how to get to the Navy Command when I suggested that we borrow the LtCol's jeep. They pointed out to me that the steering wheel was chained and padlocked. "No problem for a North American Blue Jacket" I informed them as I picked the lock with the Jeep's lug wrench, threw my duffle bag into the Jeep, and cried "All aboard for Naval Support Activity Danang."

*We stopped a couple of Marine MPs in a Jeep and asked directions to the NAVSUPACT. They told us it was called the **"white elephant"** and we followed them to it and asked how we could get to the **Mobile Base 1 (MSB 1)** on the mouth of the **Perfume River**. The Groups Op Boss sent us to a Swift that was headed north and could drop us off at the barge.*

*The boat ride to the Perfume River convinced me that I had lucked-out getting orders to PBRs and not Swifts. Swifts are the worst riding boats I have ever been to sea in. The trip was the closest I have ever been to being seasick. When we got to the mouth of the Perfume, a **LCM** showed-up to take us to the Barge. After chow we were taken into the Tactical Operations Center (TOC) where we were told that the **severity of the enemy's Tet Campaign required reinforcement of forces in the I CTZ.***

*Naval combat and support forces were **increased early in 1968**, units were deployed there from stations further south in the Mekong Delta region. These PBR units comprised Task Force CLEARWATER. The task force was charged with securing the two major waterways of the I CTZ: the **Cua Viet River and the Hue River**. The PBR element of the Hue River Security Group and Task Force CLEARWATER headquarters, were located in Tan My lagoon on **Mobile Base 1 MSB 1 which was a floating base** that consisted of large connected pontoons. Huts for berthing, messing, repair, and command and control functions were built on these pontoons.*

*To the north of Tam My Lagoon was the Tam Giang Lagoon to the south was the Cau Hai Lagoon. The Tam Giang and Cau Hai met at **Tam My**. The Perfume river flowed into these three lagoons then emptied into to the **South China Sea**. The PBR unit had quit patrolling the Perfume River after TET started. It was charged with the task of organizing the LCUs and LCMs coming up from Danang taking supplies to the LCU ramp in Hue. The first* *attempts had been disastrous and it was decided the boats would gather at* **Tam My, the unit would form them into a convoy, and provide fire support for the run to Hue.** *It worked well and continued throughout TET.*

Initially the PBRs took heavy fire from the banks of the river, but after about a week the NVA was **concentrating their fire power on the LCU and LCMs.** *We later found out the enemy units* **had been directed not fire on the little green boats because they did not seem to be hitting them.** *Well, they were hitting us with everything they had, .50 Cal, AK47, B 40s etc. The problem was everything fired at us passed right through the hull. This included the B40 rocket-propelled grenades.* **If they happened to hit the engine or some the little bit of armor plating we had it was a disaster.**

A 31-foot green boat traveling low in the water firing three .50 Cal and one Mk 60 machine gun is tough to hit. *Those .50s tended to keep the enemy heads down. Being dumped on by a .50 Cal machine gun will tend to spoil ones aim and* **quite possibly screw up your medical record.** *In addition to the convoy duty, we patrolled the Tam Giang and Cau Hay lagoons. It was mostly showing the flag and PsyOps in the form of providing food from* **US Aid, Navy Operation Hand Clasp, and medicine** *to the villages along the bank.*

The area had been under a 24-hour curfew and the villagers were unable to fish or get to market, **so we were a main food source.** *We would fish using grenades and C3 plastic explosive (AKA* **"DuPont" spinners**). *We also found you could down a lot of ducks in flock with the forward twin .50s. The villagers would stream out to us in their sampans to pick up the fish and or ducks. We would also have cooking oil, rice, and other goodies for them.*

The villagers also thought that all US military officers were **Bac-Si (Doctors).** *They would bring wounded and sick out to the boat for the Bac-Si to heal. We had very extensive field medical kits and great first aid training at Vallejo but doctors we weren't.*

Unfortunately, we could not convince those poor suffering Vietnamese villagers of that. First there was the language barrier, we had forgotten just about all the Vietnamese we had learned at Coronado. Second, we could treat a sucking gut wound, stop major bleeding, and do temporary splints, but things like menstrual cramps and the common cold etc. stumped us. So, we dispensed the greatest medicine ever made--the aspirin. We also would check in with the US Navy advisors in Cau Hay Bay and the Marine .50 Cal platoon. We would provide them with ammo medicine, C-rats, or anything else we could **scrounge, steal or cumshaw** *(bargain for).* **Because of the constant zero visibility due to fog and rain, and no ground transportation, we were their main supply line."**

After Tet, we returned to routine patrols and we were all looking for a fight. These patrols consisted of checking all sampans and junks on the river. We checked IDs, searched for evidence of VC affiliation, and weapons. **We watched the banks for any unusual activity, which was mostly the absence of villagers which meant you had VC or NVA in the area.** *We handed out Psyops material, food, gum and just tried to talk with the boat people. We also did MED CAPS (medical civic action programs) into the villages when we could get a doctor and an interpreter. On night patrols we spent most of the time drifting and eyeballing the river with our Star Light night vision device. It was all very tedious and boring.*

After my last patrol I was pulled off the river in May and told to go to **Nha Be** *to join my new unit. I was supposed to go by helo. I packed my duffel bag and was saying my goodbyes when the* **USCGC Blackhaw (WLB-390)** *steamed into the bay where we were anchored. The Blackhaw had replaced the Nettle at Sangley Point. I took the Boston Whaler out and boarded her. The crew was mostly the same when I had rode here to get my OOD Quals. I asked the CO CAPT Snyder (who was the same skipper when I was on the Nettle) what the ship was doing at Tam Mi. He told me they were going to lay some buoys in the channel to Tam Mi from the South China Sea. I asked where they were going after that. He* *spoke the words I wanted to hear. Danang. I asked if I could bum a ride.* **He said yes but I would have to drive part way--instant OOD Underway qual.** *I went back to the MSB1 to grab my duffel bag and brief case and went back to the Blackhaw. CAPT Snyder* **asked me if I knew the channel, and I told him I did. Well he wanted me on the bridge with him when they laid the buoys.**

We went out into the South China Sea, did a 180, and headed back into the bay to lay the buoys on the North side of the channel. We laid the first one, rigged another, and were going in to lay it when a Mike 8 (small boat) cut in front of us. The Captain went hard right and **aground.** *The skipper dropped the buoy hoping to lighten us enough to clear the shoal water. No joy. There we were aground on the* **lee shore of Indian country and pounding in the surf. I got on the radios and dialed in every frequency I could remember and sent out Maydays. The tide was ebbing and we were in deep kimchi.**

Another Mike 8 came by. We hailed it put a line over to him and he took a strain but to no avail. Then an EE black souped-up LCU came by. **We rigged a hawser over to it and with the Mike 8 still taking a strain, the two boats pulled us clear.** *We cleared all lines and headed into the bay close to MSB-1 and dropped the hook. The Captain said he was not going back to sea until he could get divers to inspect his hull for damage.*

Well there went my ride to Danang so I went back aboard the MSB1 and wait for a helo which took me to Red Beach. I thumbed a ride to Tenshaw and went to check into the BOQ—but "no room at the inn." I had come off of a night patrol had not had time to change and shower when this journey started. All I wanted was a hot shower, cold beer, and a rack so I headed to the Chiefs' club to see if any of my Sangley mates might be there. Sure enough, I ran into a Gunny (Gunnery Sergeant) from Marine Barracks Sangley Point who remembered me; I told him my sad story and he said that it was "No problem as they had empty racks in the Gunny's barracks and let's have a beer," which we commenced to have--several in fact, before departing to his barracks. By then it was dark the Gunny found me an empty rack and said "let's have another beer."

The barracks had a dark room that you could go in after lights out which was shortly after sundown. There a couple of guys in the room looking for some poker players. We joined them, and **played for a while when there was an explosion nearby. Someone yelled "Incoming,"** *a siren started wailing everyone grabbed their weapon and was heading for the bunkers when we heard small arms fire at the perimeter. We headed there, returned the fire, and spent the rest of the night there.*

The next morning the Gunny took me to the airport to catch a flight to Saigon. I waited around til late in the afternoon before I got a hop to Saigon. It was dark when we arrived and got into the In-country terminal. I went to the desk to ask the Air Force desk clerk how to get transportation to the Annapolis Hotel--he said there was none. I asked how I was supposed to get there he said he had no idea and that was my problem not his. About that time, **the sirens went off and we heard some explosions.** *A young Army infantry soldier who was on the plane with me asked where the air raid bunker was.* **The same smart ass told him the bunkers were for Air Force personnel only and we had to leave the terminal.**

By this time another soldier had joined us and we went outside when it had begun to rain; **great, incoming fire and rain, too.** *We couldn't see any shelter from rain or rockets. There was* **a Six-by parked by the terminal and we could crawl under it and stay dry.** *Once under, we lit up and listened to the rain and a few more rocket rounds. Then one of the soldiers posed the question: what if we fall asleep and someone starts the truck and drives off? That was a problem. The other soldier came up with the solution that he would pull the wires from the battery. Great idea kid, go for it. We popped the hood and he found the wires and pulled them. We went back under the truck and went to sleep. We woke up early the next morning as one is want to do when sleeping under a truck on asphalt with a flak jacket for a pillow and no* *chow for some time. Crawled out from under the truck and were going to replace the wires **when we noticed it was an Air Force truck and said "screw it."***

*We started looking for a ride when I spotted a bus; we hopped aboard and I got to the Annapolis just in time to catch a shuttle to **Nha Be**--wherever in the hell that was. We arrived at Nha Be and as the bus was heading down the road on the Support Activity, I spotted several of my PBR classmates. We caught-up on where everybody was and **who had and hadn't made it through the TET offensive**. Everyone wanted to know what had happened to Barry; I told them all I knew was he caught some shrapnel from an RPG 47. **We had not had a chance to talk very much about it or we just didn't want to.***

Steve Thiel CDR USNR (Retired) *US Navy*

*****Commander (Ret) Steve Thiel** grew up on a wheat farm near Ritzville WA and graduated from Washington State University and joined the Navy in 1964 via OCS. He served at USNS Sangley Point, as an Officer of the Deck Underway on *USCG Nettle (WAK-169)*, and went through Naval Inshore Operational Training Command (NIOTC) in 1967. Steve served in Vietnam during 1968-69 with *CTF Clearwater* **during the *Tet Offensive*, CTF 15 in the**

Delta region, and as an advisor to Vietnamese Navy PBRs. Steve served on amphibious ships including *USS Vermillion (LKA-109)*, *USS Inchon (LPH 12)*, as First Lieutenant on the *USS Coral Sea (CVA-43)*, Executive Officer of *USS Kiska (AE-35)*, Commanding Officer of *Special Boat Unit 22*, and retired in 1986.

Veterans Coming Home and PTSD At the end of their tours, thousands of veterans were flown back to the US and returned abruptly to a nation in chaos over Vietnam. Robert Curry spells out the situation:

*"The veterans returning home from Vietnam, Laos, and other corners of Asia **came back one by one, slipping back in the middle of the night into the country** that sent them to fight their war. Servicemen and women, anywhere in this era knew, were ordered not to wear their uniform or let others know they were in the military...*

***To survive, the Vietnam veteran went underground.** He or she hid any association with a war the country was attempting to exorcise from its soul. For decades, the VA (Veterans Administration) with the help of government cutbacks, continued to ignore the travesty this war wrought on the Vietnam Veteran. **PTSD, or Post Traumatic Stress Disorder was acknowledged a decade after Vietnam** as a defined mental diagnosis by the American Psychiatric Association. Continued shock to an individual by traumatic events such as war, would have profound impact on many veterans to function in society. It was **subtle, masking itself well** as doctors and society attempted to treat its symptoms; alcohol or drug abuse, relationship problems, anger, isolation and suicide...Finally when the problem (PTSD) was acknowledged, the vet was well underground."*[91]

Korea **In January 1968,** North Korean ships captured the American intelligence ship, ***USS Pueblo (AGER-2)*** and held the crew captive for 11 months. The North Koreans also had tried to assassinate the South Korean President the day before *Pueblo's* capture. The US quickly responded by calling up Air Force Reservists and increasing military support for South Korea. President Johnson

[91] Robert Curry, Op. cit., pp. 285-286

stated "One of our first actions after **the Pueblo incident** was to dispatch more than 350 aircraft to our air bases in South Korea and to recall to active duty selected units of the Air National Guard and Air Force Reserve to replace our strategic reserve in the United States...the North Koreans had a larger air force and we did not wish them to be tempted by that advantage."[92]

1967 Ltjg Ken Klocek (4th from right) Iwakuni *US Navy*

*Navy P-3 Pilot Ken Klocek recalls being deployed to a Navy-Marine Corp air base in Iwakuni Japan when the Pueblo was "stolen" by North Korea in 1968:

Iwakuni air base in southern Japan represented the nearest Navy/ Marine Corps Forces to the event. At the base there were P-3 Orion reconnaissance aircraft as well as US Marine Corps aircraft. Also at the base were **stockpiles of depth bombs and torpedoes for anti-submarine use.** *I presume there were also supplies of various rockets which could be launched on P-3 aircraft. At the time,* **all Navy P-3 operations were in a "peacetime" mode, in the classic "unarmed reconnaissance plane" configurations.**

At the time of the attack on the Pueblo, at nearby Iwakuni Navy/

---

[92] Lyndon B. Johnson, Op. cit., p. 535

Marine Corp base there was a P-3 Orion aircraft and **crew ready to launch in one hour** *or less and* **three P-3 Orion aircraft airborne on various surveillance/reconnaissance missions.**

I was a navigator/co-pilot in one of the P-3s which was airborne that day, January 23, 1968. *With no weapons or armament, these P-3s, including mine, would not have been able to engage North Korean forces. At best they could have reported what was occurring.* **If anybody had known! Our crew had no idea what was happening just a few air miles away.** *We landed, debriefed, and ate dinner. Other crews reported chatter on radio frequencies, but our crew heard nothing.*

Even "unarmed reconnaissance" operations that day were not in the cards, since no one at the base, nor crews in the air, knew what was happening to **Pueblo,** *just a few minutes flying time from the base.*

Later that evening I learned the news of the attack on the **Pueblo** *reached Navy Command Posts at Okinawa, but the information was not passed to us, the nearest Navy and Marine Corp air units at Iwakuni, Japan where my squadron was located!*

Eventually the Commander of the P-3 squadron was **instructed to get two airplanes/crews ready for immediate launch.** *The orders came, however, without any indication what the problem was, or what the mission might be, since the critical messages had not been forwarded to Iwakuni Command Center. Eventually the Commander heard the news of the attack on the* **Pueblo** *from a report broadcast on the Armed Forces Radio Network, a music and news station operated in English for the benefit of US service men in the Pacific.*

Even though it was almost dark, things moved quickly, as I recall. **The entire squadron was put on alert.** *Not long afterwards, Marine Corp fighter/attack jets were at the end for the runway, armed and ready to launch. Four engine P-3 Orions were readied, fueled, and armed with torpedoes and depth bombs for immediate launch.* *We had no night vision* *capability, so night operations would not have been useful for reconnaissance. Early the next day, flight operations with **armed aircraft began.***

I was assigned a schedule of 12-hour flights, with a midnight launch and a noon recovery the next day. In a few days, Patrol Squadron 48, augmented by other deployed WestPac P-3 Squadrons, began flying around the clock supporting two aircraft carriers off coast of the Korea. The base was saturated with P-3 aircraft from all over the Pacific. Aircraft covered the ramp and taxiways. The "crisis" was short-lived for me. Within a week, my squadron's scheduled deployment came to an end and my crew returned to California with a long fight via Midway Island to Moffet Field.

*PPC Ken Klocek still remembers a "FIRE IN FLIGHT and a Long Way From Home (3 hours from nowhere)"

I mentioned that I had a fire in flight when I was in the Navy...and went on to tell the story I have told many times since that flight.

I tell the story because I am so proud of the crewmen I flew with on that day. *My memory when it comes to names was never good and is worse now. I hope that by telling the story again the proper crewmen can get recognized for their professionalism at this late, late, date.*

*It was in the **Spring of 1969 while I was deployed to Adak, Alaska with Patrol Squadron 48. I was a pilot and newly-designated Aircraft Commander** in a P-3 Orion with my own crew, a not so minor achievement for a "first tour" Lieutenant.*

On a tactical flight in the direction of Petropavlovsk, Russia, a whiff of burning electrical insulation made its way to the cockpit. *During the brief discussion with the Co-pilot and Flight Engineer the fumes seem to get stronger.*

*There is no "good" time for a fire in an airplane, and **a thousand miles from an airfield and over the cold Bering sea is a very "bad" time for a fire, in my opinion.***

*It took only a few seconds and a couple more breaths that we agreed to execute the Fire in Flight Emergency checklist. I recall being in the right seat at the time and making the announcement over the speaker system. I pulled out the checklist and read the first item: "**Alert the Crew**" as I recall. I selected PA and said, "**Execute the Fire Bill. This is not a drill.**" And then provided my own response to the first item. "Crew Altered."*

I had NO idea how incredibly "Alert" they were!

*I had just started reading the second item when a crewman came to the cockpit and said something like "**We got it!**"*

*That means from my announcement to "Execute the Fire Bill" to "We got it" **was less than a minute.***

Here is why:** Leadership provided by the crew›s regularly assigned **Tactical Coordinator (TACCO) ensured that a major drill was carried out by the crew on each Tactical flight** in accordance with Squadron Operating procedures. For a "Fire in Fight Emergency," most crew members had assigned electronic bays to check, and a spare crewmember was assigned as "run-ner" or messenger under the assumption the Intercom would not work. The crew I was on **typically flew together and actually performed the drills and did not "gun deck" ("pencil-whip/ sign-off) the paperwork.

Those drills really paid off in this case.

*From the time the crew "alert" came over the speakers to the time the crewman entered the cockpit seemed like just a few seconds. I recall being incredulous that the message came to the cockpit SO FAST. **I also recall being VERY relieved, since the next check-list was labeled "Smoke and Fume Elimination" (if lucky), followed by "Ditching."***

*In this case, "We got it" meant that the **Radio Operator had left his seat, started checking his assigned electronic bays, found the overheated electronics (a TACAN/Navigation*** *transmitter/receiver), broke the safety wires, spun-off the hold downs, slid the hot TACAN unit of the rack, and used his pocket knife with a screwdriver blade to loosen several screws on the case, and take off the top cover, while another crew member stood by with a fire extinguisher.*

As far as I know, it was a one hundred percent NATOPS (Standard Operating Procedures) compliant evolution and **they had done it with lightning speed while we were over the Bering Sea and 3 hours from nowhere.**

WHAT HAPPENED? The TACAN unit had been replaced the day/ night before. Due the heat generated by the TACAN Receiver/ Transmitter, the unit had its own cool air supply provided by a flexible hose hooked to the aircraft equipment bay cooling system. The air supply had to be attached at the rear of the unit as it was slid into the electronics rack. In this case the tube was not attached or had been crunched and was not effective. **It took a few hours, but without cooling air the TACAN eventually overheated and started a classic "melt-down."**

WHO WAS ON THE CREW? I wish I could recall. **The Radio operator was a Chief Petty Officer, had a private or commercial pilot's license, and could fly the P-3 better than I could straight and level,** *but I can't recall his name. The other pilot was probably* **Paul Yakubek** *(now deceased), but I don't have a crew list to help jog my memory. Although* **"Radio" was the man on the spot, it was clearly a CREW evolution.**

To the crew this probably wasn't a "big deal" like a mid-air or ditching, **but to me, totally dependent on their actions, it WAS a big deal and a huge relief when it was over.**

Recounting the story today for the umpteenth time, I said, "Those guys deserve a medal!"

Well, they deserve more recognition than they got at the time (none). *If I had been more experienced in such things, I* *would have worked on Letters of Commendation or at least a Meritorious Mast with the Commanding Officer.*

Almost fifty years later, and almost fifty years too late, I want that TACCO and crew to know how grateful I was then and now for their quick and efficient action.

Truk MEDEVAC: Unscheduled, Unauthorized Medical Evacuation 50 years ago -- July 15, 1968

*I remember there were either two or three crews and aircraft sent to Guam on short notice. I DO recall their being **four officers packed into one Un-air-conditioned BOQ room**. The climate was very "tropical" (hot and humid) since Guam is closer to the equator than Manila, PI. We presumed that Air Force pilots over at Anderson AFB were living in luxury with air conditioning, and eating lobster and steak, with nurses and school teachers for company. I still think that was true!*

*We were sent to Guam on a classified mission that was repeatedly postponed. While waiting, we were **recruited to do an annual "inventory" or "survey" of what was then a U.N. Protectorate under US administration**, or something similar.*

*We had almost no instructions. Nothing written, no forms, and no records that I recall. We would fly to the various islands, often with only a few dozen, or few hundred inhabitants, and do a "fly over." We were to report an unusual or suspicious activity, or similar words. Of course to me, flying over tropical islands at 200 feet (the height of a 20 story building) everything was "unusual." **Unfortunately, flying by at 200 MPH didn't give us a chance to see much. But of course the island inhabitants saw us -- a four engine aircraft the size of an airliner.** And they came out to see us; I recall at the smaller islands, if we made a second pass, the beaches and shallow water would be filled with locals waving at us as we flew by. It was some of the most "recreational" flying I did as a Navy pilot. There wasn't much for the 10-man crew to day, and even the usually busy navigator had little navigation* *to do, and only minimum logs to keep. The typically burdened Navigator merely gave a rough heading for the next island to the pilots and keep a rough log, and often came to the cockpit to look out at the blue and endless Pacific with the pilots.*

The entire time were operated doing the survey, we never had much of a flight plan, other than "We going in the direction of Saipan or Yap, and we'll be back later."

On the day of the Medical Evacuation, we were on a zig-zag course checking islands enroute back to Guam in time for dinner. As part of the flight we over-flew the island of Truk (now called Chuuk). At the time Truk was known to historians as the location of a World War Two naval battle, but was mostly undeveloped, and not on anybody's list as a "must see" destination.

As we flew around the coastline, we checked in on the only radio frequency we had for the island's airport. Since we were not on a flight plan, we called "Truk operations" (whoever they were) as a courtesy in case there were any other airplanes in the area. We told them who we were and where we going.

Fifteen to twenty minutes after we had passed over Truk and briefly chatted on the radio, we got a call from "Truk Operations." (As luck would have it, one radio was still tuned to their frequency, since we had no reason to change it.)

They asked if we would return and Medevac child who needed medical care not available on the island. Somebody at the local medical clinic must have heard us fly overhead and made a quick phone call to the airport. *And that resulted in the radio call to us, politely asking if we could be of assistance. Looking back in the event, there was some really fast thinking by somebody or several people on the ground. Fortunately, we had not re-tuned our radios to another frequency, and they called us before we got out of range, but just barely.*

Air Force pilots would have had to call Washington for permission, but a couple of Navy P-3 pilots said, "Heck, yes.

Why not?" *(After we checked our fuel, to make sure we could fly back to Truk, make an approach and landing, take off and get back to Guam/Navy Agana and land with reserve). The was virtually no Command structure involved, we were on the most "independent operations" of our career, there was no one to give or deny "permission" and our Commanding Officer was several thousand miles away in California. So we turned around and headed back to Truk!*

*I was a senior co-pilot at the time, and might soon be promoted to Aircraft Commander, but lacked exposure and experience when it came to decision making. The **Aircraft Commander at the time generously took it upon himself to train me, or try, to make the types of decisions I would eventually have to make.** He provided very little coaching and let me make many of the decisions during that weeks we operated out of Guam.*

Unfortunately, on that day the return to the island of Truk and the landing did not go well.

We had some publications which had data on the airport at Truk. We discovered the runway was rather short at about 5,000 feet. We knew that the runway length was easily within the operating range of the aircraft, but neither of us had actually landed on a runway that short. And we talked about the runway length being a factor in the approach and landing. The runway both began and ended at the water's edge, which gave the situation a certain "gravitas."

As a result, I spooked myself into thinking it was a really short runway that required special techniques.

*I made a fairly normal approach over the water. As we were about to touch down, and being a bit worried about stopping on a "short" runway, I cut the power while still a little above the runway. **A "cut" in a turboprop means a disaster will follow. And it did. A hard landing.** I really planted it. After the hard landing, and with a clear view of the blue ocean at the end of the runway, I quickly brought the four large* *turbo-props into reverse thrust. This means, four 13-foot diameter fans hooked to 4000 horsepower engines began to blow a LOT of air forward of the aircraft.*

Bad news quickly followed. We understood that the runway was short. But the hard landing was a couple seconds ago. History. **What we did not understand was that the runway was not paved. The runway surface was crushed coral.**

The high velocity air from the reverse thrust kicked up the loose coral, and then the coral smartly headed for the engine intakes. (No matter how much reverse the prop puts up, the engines gotta have air!)

I'm not sure who was first to realize reverse thrust was both a REALLY BAD, BAD IDEA, and reverse thrust was not needed to stop the plane. Getting back to "neutral" thrust and keeping coral rocks out of the engine intake was an immediate requirement.

We were 1,000 - 2,000 feet from the end of the runway when we stopped...Of course, the **"end" of the runway is where the ocean began.**

After getting the boy, his mother, and maybe a medical person on board, we made it back to NAS Agana with no problem. We called ahead and told Agana we had a medical problem on board, and let the ground folks take it from there.

I don't recall any feed-back on the child, but we never got into trouble, nor did we get an "attaboy" for our diversion. We just had an entry in our log books: "GUM-TRUK-GUM, (Guam-Truk-Guam)" a lesson in landing on crushed coral, and a few memories.

*** Ken Klocek was commissioned through NROTC at the University of Rochester in 1964. After pilot and navigator training, he flew sea planes at NAS North Island, San Diego and later P-3 Orion aircraft based at NAS Moffett Field, California while assigned to Patrol Squadron 48. During that time, he deployed to Japan,

Guam, and Adak, in the Aleutian Islands. After a second tour as an S-2 Navy flight instructor, Ken left the Navy to pursue a career as a commercial pilot. He rounded out his active duty in the Navy with another 20 years in the Navy Reserve.

"Going In" or Avoiding Service and Vietnam A Senior in my high school graduated and went straight into the Army and then directly to Vietnam. While he was there, he ordered a hot Chevy *Super Sport 396 Coupe* to be delivered to a small-town dealership so he could pick it up when he got back; I saw him driving it like a bat out of hell. **He was like many young men from rural and poorer parts of the US who mostly volunteered or accepted the Draft and took the brunt of the war.**

However, in many parts of the US, sympathetic anti-war doctors granted medical deferments which created more pressure on poorer kids who didn't have the connections. These "Grunts" –and their families-- bore the burden of Vietnam and should be always REMEMBERED for their sacrifices.

Few Northeast college grads volunteered for the military during 1968-72 which was marked by anti-war demonstrations, anti-ROTC protests, the March on Washington, and the resignation of President Johnson.

*I started with 77 NROTC Midshipmen in 1968 and only 17 of us were finally commissioned in 1972.

In the Fall of 1968, our new NROTC Marine Major had just come to Cornell from the siege of **Khe Sanh.** Anti-war protestors threw purple paint balloons at a Marine Major recruiter from Syracuse at his table and later, occupied part of the NROTC and **painted flowers on the 5"/38 WWII naval gun.** One day at drill, the **SDS** (Students for a Democratic Society) and allies planned to try to start fights with Midshipmen, so the Marine Major pre-briefed us to form-up in battalion formation and then gave order to disperse, so no one got caught on camera fighting while in uniform which is what the demonstrators wanted.

In the spring of **1969 after several anti-war protests**, many of the "Regular" scholarship midshipmen quit and suddenly there were scholarships available, so I applied for one and with this *windfall tuition also applied to the College of Arts and Sciences. I was interviewed by an Assistant Dean with grey brush-cut hair. Since all students had long hair then, he almost fell over when I walked in with my short haircut and said "Are you in ROTC?" and I said "Yes Sir, I am." To which he said "G_D_It!* **I was in one of Patton's first tanks across the Rhine River and I don't think we should have stopped rolling east until we got to Moscow, do you?** *And I said "Uh--No Sir, I don't" ---and I was suddenly admitted to College of Arts and Sciences.*

Only two college students I knew during 1968-1972 volunteered for the military: one became a tanker pilot and the other became a Marine JAAG. Many Northeastern college grads did not serve—they let someone else go and the officer corps tipped disproportionately to more conservative areas of the US which contributed to long-term effects on the military.

There were a lot of ways to get deferments to avoid Vietnam or the Service via college, having children, etc and many used their connections to find some deal to avoid service and theology school suddenly become very popular. **Some politicians received deferments (or managed to obtain deferments, special deals, special handling for their kids) to avoid military service.**

Prominent individuals who managed to avoid military service and Vietnam in various ways include: President Clinton, Vice President Biden, Senator Schumer, Senator Sanders, Senator Lieberman, Mayor Bloomberg, President Trump, Governor Romney, OMB Director Stockman, Speaker DeLay, Attorney General Ashcroft, Limbaugh, O'Reilly, Nugent, Springsteen and *"chickenhawks"* like Vice President Cheney, Wolfowitz, Perle, Rove, Speaker Gingrich, Mayor Giuliani, and others.

Well-off young men had access to **college deferments** and often **sympathetic anti-war doctors** who could certify they were medically unfit for the military. This placed higher pressures on **poorer men** who had to serve in Vietnam combat units and had **high casualty rates**.

Tens of thousands of Americans went to **Canada** to avoid Vietnam service. I know families who planned to help their sons go to Canada if they were drafted. **In 1977 President Carter pardoned the *draft dodgers*** and about half of them stayed in Canada.[93]

The Draft Lottery Bowing to wide-spread opposition to the Vietnam Draft, President Nixon amended the *Military Selective Service Act of 1967* and initiated the first *Draft Lottery* on December 1, 1969 for men born between 1944 to 1950. Unfortunately, the plastic capsules bearing the numbers equating to each birthday date starting with January, February, March etc. **were not mixed thoroughly, so those with birthdates in latter months of the year were disproportionately picked.** This is how my friend, a gifted chemical engineer born in December, suddenly had to find a spot in the military and so he became a soil tester in the Army Reserve.

Ltjg Lidstone working a sextant aboard *USS Shreveport (LPD-12)*

* Herrick K. Lidstone, Jr. recalls how the Draft Lottery changed his life:

Before going to Cornell University in August 1967, I applied for and was actually accepted to the U.S. Naval Academy at Annapolis. A family friend talked me out of going. My father (who served with the 79th Infantry Division, landed on Normandy at

---
[93] John Hagan *Northern Passage: American Vietnam War Resisters in Canada,* Harvard University Press 2001 pp 167, 242

127

D+6, and was in combat from then until VE Day) was incredibly upset – and not just because of the tuition difference. Thus, I ended up at Cornell.

*Cornell was an interesting place at the time **including anti-war protestors, women's rights, the black liberation front, and die-hard conservatives. Roman Catholic Father Daniel Berrigan** (for a time on the FBI's list of the ten-most wanted criminals because of his anti-Vietnam war activities) was the assistant director of the Cornell University United Religious Work (1966-1970) and frequently preached against the war. Among other things, Father Berrigan and six other priests (including his brother Phillip Berrigan) used napalm to destroy 378 draft files in Catonsville, Maryland on May 17, 1968. **Protests against the war, for women's rights and against racism were regular occurrences at Cornell from 1968-1970.***

*I was included in the **first draft lottery (Monday, December 1, 1969)**. I remember sitting around the television at Sigma Nu fraternity with a number of brothers (I was a member) watching a life-defining event. And we knew it. There was, of course, beer all around. One of my brothers was selected early – I do not remember which number. We toasted his luck; I was second – **September 10, 1949 got me #71** – coincidentally the year of my Cornell graduation. The Fall Creek House was giving **50% discounts on drinks to anyone under 100** – it was good that the drinking age was 18 at the time. I remember going to Fall Creek House, but sure do not remember walking back up the hill. I do not think I bought a drink all night.*

*My father offered his congratulations; my mother was panicked. As I recall, I spent Christmas break with a classmate in Colombia, South America. When I returned on my way to Cornell, my mother had an appointment for me with a **doctor guaranteed to give me a medical deferment at a cost I did not know**, but likely was more than I could afford. I was able to avoid that appointment but during spring break I went into Manhattan to be examined by the doctor who (as I recall) found heart and lung*

*problems – either one of which would have served me well for **my
4-F medical deferment**. I thanked him, took his report home,
showed it to Mom and Dad, and then tore it up. I remember
Dad smiling; Mom was very upset.*

*1970 was an interim election year. I worked for **Senator Jacob
Javits (R-NY) as an intern the summer of 1970. My job was
primarily national health insurance – being sponsored by
Senator Javits and Senator Ted Kennedy ((D-MA).** Our offices
worked well together, but as history will attest, national health
insurance went nowhere.*

*The **fall semester 1970 at Cornell was quite disjointed** as the
mid-term elections were the focus of much anxiety and protest
as a result of Richard Nixon's presidency and Spiro Agnew's vice
presidency. Cornell administrators recommended that interested
students focus on public service during the campaign. At Senator
Javits' recommendation, I worked on the **Charles Goodell sena-
torial campaign** – Governor Rockefeller had appointed Goodell
to fill **Bobby Kennedy's unexpired term following his June
1968 assassination**. James Buckley easily won that election.
(The NFL commissioner Roger Goodell is Charles Goodell's son.)*

*On election day, I reported to the Brooklyn Navy Yard for my
enlistment physical and then returned to Cornell for the end-
of-semester classes. With Senator Javits' help, I had applied for
**Naval OCS. I intended to "dodge the draft and join the Navy."
The family joke was that I was not going to move to Canada
because I had too many cousins there.** (Mom had found her
sense of humor again – the cousins were all from her family, who
moved to Toronto decades before, and then spread out.)*

*My application for Naval OCS was languishing, and in February/
March 1971 as I recall, I received my notice for my draft physical.
Three of us were to report to the Syracuse, NY, draft station early
one morning in April (as I recall). I do remember someone saying
that if we drank enough red wine, the urine would come out red
and they would think it to be blood in the urine. **I can assure you***

that did not work.

*After graduation in May 1971, a friend and I hopped into his car and took a driving trip around the perimeter of the United States – down the east coast, around the Gulf Coast, and then to Las Vegas, Los Angeles and San Francisco. In New Orleans, I spoke to my father who told me that I had **received my admission to OCS, but I had also received my draft notice.** He said that if I flew back to New York and enlisted into the Navy, they would hold my OCS class and it would avoid my being drafted. That was a no-brainer, so I flew from San Antonio, Texas back to New York, enlisted in the Navy, and flew back to San Antonio to finish our trip. My OCS class started in January 1972 (Tuesday, January 4th as I recall). I reported for duty. My WWII Army-combat veteran father's advice was:*

1. You cannot dig foxholes on the deck of a ship; and

2. Keep your eyes, ears, nose, and bowels open, and your mouth shut.

*I was assigned to the **USS Shreveport (LPD-12)** in May 1972 and spent my entire active duty on the Shreveport, stationed out of Norfolk Naval Base, Virginia. I never saw Vietnam or the Pacific theatre. The Shreveport:*

- *was in the English Channel and the North Atlantic on a six-week cruise with Naval Academy midshipmen (summer 1972),*
- *was assigned to the Sixth Fleet as the Mediterranean Amphibious Ready Group (**MARG**, January into July 1973), and*
- *was assigned to COMPHIBLANT for a number of four- to six-week cruises in the Caribbean as the "Caribbean Amphibious Ready Group" (**CARG**).*

*The MARG and CARGs generally consisted of **five or six ships consisting of LPDs, LSDs, and LSTs, and the Shreveport was usually the flagship except when an LHA was involved.** By my calculation, the **Shreveport spent substantially more time at sea during my three years on board (May 1972-May 1975) than in port.** A young married officer had two children born while* *we were on deployment. The skipper tried to get him back for the second birth, but the baby came early. From the perspective of a young, single, unattached officer, I had no complaints.*

*Especially during the early part of my Naval career, I was considered the **SLJO – sh__y little jobs officer.** When something needed to be done, I got assigned. As a result, when the skipper had to detail some officers for a few days to the HMS. Ark Royal (from which Prince Charles then flew helicopters), **I was volunteered.** When he needed to send an officer to serve with the Italian Navy as a liaison officer, I was volunteered for the duration. When we had Turkish Marines on board to transport from Izmir to operations on Cyprus (where the Greeks did not like the Turks), I was their liaison officer on ship and received calls at all hours of the day and night to solve problems. When an officer had to volunteer for shore patrol in Palma, Mallorca (Spain), Naples (Italy), and other ports, I was volunteered. In the Caribbean I was the liaison to Brazilian, Venezuelan, and Colombian ships. I told my son who retired after eleven years from the Army's 82nd Airborne with medical issues (as an E-6) that **I started off as the worse O-1 (Navy Ensign – Army Second Lieutenant) possible – one who thought that he knew something, but in reality had not a clue.***

*At some point following our Mediterranean cruise, I became "competent" and went to training as, and took over the duties of the **Combat Information Center Officer,** which carried with it responsibility for electronic warfare and intelligence components. (I think that it had to do with a new skipper and ops officer reporting on board.) I was no longer the SLJO. We participated in a number of practice amphibious assaults which were exciting experiences, landing the U.S. marines by landing craft and helicopter. I became **a pretty good assault landing officer** – directing the boats and helicopters for coordinated and timely landings. As amphibious assault ships, our armament was laughable - 3 inch, .50 caliber "pea shooters". We never fired our guns in anger – only at targets.*

I did run into the Soviets – where our Squadron Commodore

*(COMPHIBRON, we were the flagship) almost caused an international incident – resolved by my Operations Officer (I was CIC, EW, and Intelligence). We were on deployment in the Caribbean (1974) when a Soviet AGI was traveling in and out of our five-ship formation. [My recollection is that the Marines were off of our ships on an exercise, and it was just the Navy dealing with the AGI.] The AGI was the Soviet's intelligence collector; it looked like a fishing boat but for its impressive array of electronic sensors. Normally communications underway were kept to a minimum or were secured. In this case, however, our Commodore on the flag bridge below the main bridge was getting more and more irritated at the near-collisions he believed were being caused by the **AGI's weaving throughout our formation**. He was communicating with everyone up the chain of command **to get permission to blow the AGI out of the water**, and not all of the communications were secured. My operations officer and I, the Shreveport's communications officer, and many enlisted men in the two units heard many of the communications and we reported them to our skipper. **The good news is that no permission was granted.***

*On his own, our Commodore **decided to "scare" the AGI** by ordering our five-ship amphibious squadron to General Quarters and having each ship train their small (3" .50 cal.) guns on the AGI and lock on with their fire control radar. All of this, of course, was exactly what the AGI wanted--imagine the **trove of electronic intelligence that it received from the constant communication from the flag bridge and our fire control radar.***

*After a few minutes, one of my electronic warfare (EW) petty officers reported to CICO (the Combat Information Center Officer – that was me): "detection of Kynda class radar at 030 [or whatever]"; a few minutes later, "detection of second Kynda class radar at 045 [or so]"; a few minutes later, "detection of Kresta class radar at 015 (or so)." I remember they were close on the radar screen. **Kyndas and Krestas were then modern Soviet missile cruisers.***

Of course, we reported each detection to the flag bridge. Not too long later, the EW petty officer came back and reported "all three Soviets now have their fire control radar searching for us." About the same time, the lookouts on the signal bridge reported sighting three Soviet cruisers at about the same coordinates. Our Commodore was panicking, or at least that is how it seemed to me, and he again was trying to get direction from the Atlantic Fleet commanders. All of the other activity in the area must have broken-up our radio transmissions.

*The next communication from electronic warfare was: "**All Soviet radar locked.**" My Operations Officer told me to carry that message personally to the Commodore. The flag bridge (one deck below the ship's bridge) was anything but quiet. The Commodore was shouting orders, and most of them contradictory. I gave him my report and left.*

*As I was climbing the ladder up to the ship's bridge and the Combat Information Center right behind it, the Commodore's executive officer called up to the CIC and asked my boss, the ship's Operations Officer to come down to the flag bridge. According to what he later told me, when the **Ops Officer got to the flag bridge, the Commodore turned over command of the entire squadron to our Ops Officer (not to his own Executive Officer), and retired to his stateroom.***

*Taking command, the Ops Officer gave the order to stow the guns and retire from General Quarters. He also ordered all available **sailors on all ships of the squadron to report to the decks and wave with smiles to the AGI.** The Soviet sailors came on the AGI's deck too, waiving with equally large smiles. **As soon as our fire control radar was off, the Soviet fire control radar was turned off. The three Soviet cruisers, which had come over the horizon, turned and went back to whatever exercises they had been doing.***

*That would have been **1974** by my recollection. Much more important things were going on elsewhere in the world; that was* *my little piece of action. My claim to fame in the Navy was that I was **among the first to receive the Surface Warfare Officer Badge** when it was introduced into the Navy in 1975 – just before I left active duty. It was intended to give insignia to those of us not entitled to Aviator's "Wings" or Submariner's "Dolphins." We jokingly referred to them as **"Water Wings" and were proud to have earned them.***

***Herrick K. Lidstone, Jr.** is a 1971 graduate of Cornell University College of Arts and Sciences. Herrick attended Officer Candidate School (OCS) in Newport, Rhode Island, starting in January 1972 and was commissioned an Ensign in May 1972. Herrick was immediately assigned to the *U.S.S. Shreveport* (LPD-12), an amphibious landing platform dock - part of the United States' "Gator Navy." Herrick started as a deck officer on the *Shreveport*, became the ship's administrative officer through the MARG, and became Combat Information Center, Electronic Warfare, and Intelligence officer in late-1973 or early-1974. Herrick finished his active duty after a CARG cruise in May 1975. After active duty, Herrick served in the Reserves for seven years while attending law school at the University of Colorado, Boulder, and starting the practice of law and starting a family. Herrick was promoted to Lieutenant Commander (USNR-R) before his retirement from reserve duty in March 1982. Herrick continues the practice of law, has taught at both the University of Colorado and the University of Denver, has written three law-related books, and has more than 30 published articles on various legal subjects. Some of his more recent papers are published on the social sciences research network, https://ssrn.com/author=802201.

Vietnam was a turning point for Americans' general trust in their government's foreign and defense policies and was exceptionally disruptive in social, political, military, and economic contexts. Allies, including the Australians and South Koreans who contributed much to the war effort had mixed views. However, author Peter Edwards states that "That doesn't mean there isn't a debate over the war. Defenders support the view, famously expressed by **Singapore's founding father Lee Kuan Yew, that by delaying the fall of Saigon from 1965 to 1975 the Western commitment gave potential dominoes, like Singapore, Malaysia, Thailand and Indonesia, 10 years to strengthen their political and economic resilience.** Critics insist that the cost, in blood, treasure and political credibility, was too high."[94]

I note that was easy for Lee Kuan Yew to say since it was America and its allies (Australia and Korea) who fought that paid the price of over 58,000 dead and the South Vietnamese lost hundreds of thousands to ensure Asian political and economic resilience.

+++CPL Bob Schampier USMC

Marine CPL Bob Schampier was one of the thousands of Americans who stepped-up to volunteer for Vietnam. I looked up to him; we baled hay together on our farm in upstate New York before he enlisted in the Marines in 1966. Bob was part of a **Combined Action Platoon (CAP)** *assigned to a small village called Hoa Phu in Quang Nam Province north of Da Nang. In the morning of January 6, 1968 his small unit was mortared, rocketed, and assaulted by superior forces.*

Bob, 4 other Marines, and a Navy Corpsman were killed and 3 Marines were wounded. He had been in Vietnam less than 4 months. **Bob Schampier was one of the very best--he and the 58,000 Americans who died during Vietnam should never be forgotten.**

Marine General Lew Walt paid tribute to the **CAPs:** *"Of all our innovations in Vietnam none was as successful, as lasting in effect, or as useful for the future as the Combined Action Program (CAP).*[95]

---

[94] Peter Edwards, *What Was Australia Doing in Vietnam?, The New York Times,* August 4, 2017

[95] Lewis W. Walt *Strange War, Strange Strategy: A General's Report on the War in Vietnam,* Funk and Wagnalls New York 1970 p. 105

PART II
Naval Cold War Operations

S5G Submarine Nuclear Prototype Plant Idaho National Lab   *US Navy*

Chapter 10
US and Soviet Navy Expansion

After years of intense engineering work by thousands of civilian and naval personnel, the first submarine nuclear deterrent patrol was carried out in 1960 by *USS George Washington (SSBN-598)* with 16 *Polaris* missiles (2500 NM range). *SSBN* stands for *"submarine ballistic missile nuclear-powered."* Eventually the Navy operated 41 Submarine-Launched Ballistic Missile (SLBM) submarines. **The Soviets fielded SLBMs in 1963.** Early inertial positioning and guidance were still a work in progress, so early SSBNs and SLBMs were not as accurate as ICBMs which remained the US' primary nuclear strike vehicles.

*National Energy Labs engineer Hank Zeile discusses "The Navy Goes Nuclear"

"The main function of atomic energy should be "turning the world's wheels and driving its ships." Naval Research Laboratory Scientist **Robert Gunn, December 13, 1945** *Testimony before the Special Senate Committee on Atomic Energy*

The Nuclear Navy was essential, actually indispensable, in the nation's defense posture during the Cold War; especially so the nuclear-powered submarines. A nuclear-powered submarine has the **advantages of stealth, speed and unlimited range of operations in any ocean**. *Its operation, submerged and undetected, is limited only by the supplies it carries to keep its crew well fed and healthy. Early on in the Cold War it was realized,* **by both sides, that a ballistic missile submarine (SSBN) is an excellent, and one can argue the most useful, delivery system for nuclear weapons.** *For the United States, it was the* **most** *reliable and stealthy member in the Triad—land based missiles, strategic bombers and nuclear submarines—of nuclear weapons delivery systems. Likewise, **nuclear powered aircraft carriers have advantages unmatched by conventionally powered carriers—speed and unlimited range without dependence on propulsion fuel supply.***

*While the early naval nuclear reactor cores had a relatively limited—3 to 4 year—operating life and refueling took the vessel out of service for a prolonged time, as time went on core life kept increasing. Today, naval nuclear cores **have a life in excess of 30 plus** years and it's expected that with continued development lifetime **can be increased to 40 years**; essentially the lifetime of the naval vessel.*

So, how did the Navy get into nuclear propulsion for its fleet?

Before *the atomic bomb (A-bomb) ended WWII in the Pacific,* **the Navy recognized the potential of nuclear energy.** *Two scientists from the **Naval Research Laboratory, Robert Gunn and Philip Abelson, met with Professor Enrico Fermi to discuss its potential use to propel submarines.** While using nuclear energy for this purpose looked promising, the two Navy men also recognized that a **completely new technology would have to be invented.** The task seemed daunting but, if it could be done, it would be a major breakthrough in naval warfare–a true submersible weapons system.*

Three days later, *Gunn and his boss met with the Chief of Navy's Bureau of Steam Engineering, and proposed an evaluation of a "fission chamber" that would generate steam to propel submarines. Shortly thereafter, the **expenditure of a very modest sum was authorized to do a feasibility study.** Gunn submitted his report four months before the **famous letter from Einstein** to President Roosevelt recommended the development of the A-bomb. Obviously, Gunn's recommendation did not carry the same weight, as no one at the Navy Department ran with it to the President. **They were not even aware, and would not be for several more years, of***

Einstein's letter nor the vast project it set in motion. However, the Navy brass did authorize **continued low-level activity to investigate nuclear propulsion.** *The lack of top-level interest was probably because, after all, the* **Navy brass had a war to win and they had neither spare cash nor time to spend listening to some "hair-brained" ideas from a couple of their research scientists**. *It was not until the power of the atom was demonstrated at Hiroshima and Nagasaki that they finally got the message.*

By the end of 1945, they were pushing for rapid development of nuclear propulsion. *Since all the practical knowledge they needed was tied up in* **General Grove's Manhattan Project**, *they insisted that Groves let them get involved. The General Electric Company, a prime contractor to Grove's Manhattan Project at the Hanford plutonium production facilities, as part of its contract, established a government-owned research facility in Schenectady, NY to pursue fundamental research for the development of nuclear power. It was at this facility the navy funded GE to evaluate nuclear propulsion for destroyers.*

After a careful evaluation, **GE started working with sodium as a coolant for the Navy's reactor**. *Even though GE had gained significant nuclear physics and engineering experience from their operation at Hanford Washington, nuclear propulsion was a new ball game and the* **design of a small and safe reactor plant to fit within the confines of a destroyer was slow going. One for a submarine was even more challenging.**

Captain Hyman G. Rickover, a seasoned Engineering Duty Officer *was determined to be part of the navy's nuclear program. Soon after the work started in Schenectady,* **Captain Albert G. Mumma, Head of Machinery Design Division of Bureau of Ships, chose 5 Navy officers and 3 Navy civilians to participate in a reactor design study project at General Grove's Oak Ridge Tennessee Facility.** *Though he was not 1 of the 5 selected, Rickover through this connection to Grove's Deputy, Col. Kenneth D. Nicholls, was able to* **participate in the design study–the "Daniel's Project."** *The Navy personnel assigned to Oak Ridge were assigned* *to the project as individuals, not as part of a Navy team. However, Rickover was the senior officer there and quickly established himself as the leader of the 'Navy Team.'*

Eventually, the Daniel's Project didn't go to completion, but it did provide much useful nuclear physics and engineering information to the participants and the Navy team probably gained the most benefit from their Oak Ridge experience.

By that time, there were a number of 'Navy spokesmen for nuclear power' and **Rickover was not one of them. Rickover's big break came when Colonel Nicholls asked him to review a draft report on the Navy's interest in nuclear power.** *With the help of one of the officers on the Oak Ridge assignment,* **he rewrote the report.** *In its new version,* **the report, without providing any real technical basis, stated that the first nuclear powered ship could be built in 5 to 8 years and in 10 to 16 years nuclear power could power all types of Navy ships.** *This report, now known as* **the 'Rickover Report,'** *received a* **wide circulation** *within the naval establishment and gave* **Rickover the recognition to become the sole spokesman for naval nuclear propulsion.** *With Rear Admiral Solberg's support,* **Rickover was assigned to Washington as Admiral Mill's Special Assistant for Nuclear Matters.**

Ten days before his tour ended as Chief of Naval Operations, **Admiral Nimitz recommended to the Secretary of the Navy that the Navy start a Nuclear Propulsion Program.** *Over the next few months, the Navy and the Atomic Energy Commission (AEC) worked out an arrangement where the* **newly established Argonne National Laboratory (ANL) would take the lead to develop a reactor for the Navy.** *Six month later, Admiral Mills appointed* **Rickover to be the Navy/AEC liaison to ANL and he was also put in charge of the newly established Naval Reactors Branch** *in the Bureau of Ships. Soon Rickover maneuvered the AEC to appoint him as Deputy Director for Naval Reactor Development in the AEC organization.* **This double appointment, in the Navy and AEC organizations, would eventually permit**

him to operate independently of both organizations. *His immediate concern was what to do about the ANL lead for naval reactor development?*

Rickover recognized that unless he could effect a change in the Argonne assignment he would have little chance to influence the development of navy's reactor. Since Zinn's priority was the ***development of a 'breeder reactor,'*** *Rickover had his boss, Admiral Mills argued that the AEC's emphasis was nuclear weapons production and breeder reactors and that the Navy's reactor would be a back-burner operation if its development was left with ANL[96]. The argument was convincing and, not wanting to be left behind, the Navy authorized Rickover to independently turn to industry.*

The Navy already had General Electric under contract working on a sodium-cooled reactor. Now, ***Rickover turned to Westinghouse Electric Corporation, GE's major competitor, and had them organize a brand new laboratory, the Bettis Atomic Power Laboratory,*** *to design a reactor with water as the heat transfer and neutron moderating medium. Later, he also engaged a third major power engineering company, the* ***Combustion Engineering Corporation*** *at Windsor, Connecticut to work on a* ***water-cooled reactor for a small attack submarine.***

By then ***GE*** *was constructing a new laboratory,* ***the Knolls Atomic Power Laboratory (KAPL), in Niskayuna, New York.*** *There, KAPL would consolidate all the facilities performing nuclear work, spread throughout various locations around Schenectady, into one new facility. Initially GE was working under contract for to the Manhattan Engineering District, but in 1947 after the Atomic Energy Commission (AEC) was formed, GE's contract was transferred to the AEC.* ***Later, KAPL became a laboratory fully dedicated to the Navy's nuclear program.***

By late 1947, KAPL recommended sodium coolant for nuclear submarine propulsion.

Using sodium as a medium to transfer heat from the reactor

[96] Walter Zinn was Argonne National Laboratory's first director (1946-1956)

to the steam generator offered a significantly smaller reactor plant. GE reasoned that the Navy's interest was a small, simple and efficient reactor operating at high temperatures and generating superheated steam. **Technically it made perfect sense but it would turn out to be an engineering nightmare.** *Bettis was chartered to design a water-cooled reactor, which turned out to be a much simple engineering task.*

To deliver on his 5-year promise, Rickover needed competition so, he funded the design and construction of submarines using both reactor concepts *and had them built as quickly as possible.* **The first nuclear-powered submarine was proposed in the Navy's 1952 budget.** *At the same time, ground was broken at the National Reactor Testing Station (NRTS) in Idaho for its prototype.*

Rickover was so confident in his ability to get the job done on schedule that 3 years earlier he had set the date for the **first nuclear submarine to be "underway" on January 1, 1955.** *However, its land-based prototype reactor (S1W Mark 1) would go critical much earlier. The schedule for the prototype plant to go 'critical' was set for a year ahead of the first submarine so that it could be fully tested and whatever problems showed up could be corrected. The design changes could then be incorporated in the first submarine before it slid down the ways.* **USS Nautilus (SSN-571), the first nuclear powered submarine, powered by Bettis designed reactor put to sea on nuclear power on January 17, 1955, missing Rickover's schedule by little more than two weeks.**

But why in Idaho? The Atomic Energy Act of 1946, *which shifted the government's nuclear work to civilian control, created a civilian agency, the Atomic Energy Commission, to administer the nuclear policy of the United States. The new agency, headquartered in Washington, now managed both classified military as well as non-classified civilian applications of nuclear technology. To keep its military secrets safe, the Act also created a* **Joint Committee on Atomic Energy (JCAE) in Congress,** *whose job was to provide policy direction and propose the budget for the AEC. This in effect* *kept the entire enterprise wholly within the purview of a small number of Congressmen, excluding all others in Congress from the classified details of AEC's business. In addition, the Act established a Committee on Reactor Safeguards, which would now weigh in on the question of where to locate the first reactors.* **After some deliberation, they recommended that first reactors be built and tested at a remote site.**

After the AEC organized the Division of Reactor Development, one of its first tasks was to locate a suitable remote site that met the Reactor Safeguards Committee's criteria. After evaluating all existing government facilities that met the criteria, it settled on the **Naval Proving Ground in southeast Idaho.**

Shortly after the start of WWII, the Sixth Supplemental National Defense Appropriations Act authorized the construction of a **Naval Ordinance Plant in Pocatello, Idaho.** *Along with the plant, where the large naval guns were to be built as well as refurbished, there was a need for a firing range remote enough to avoid hitting anyone when the guns fired a projectile at a target thirty miles away. After the war ended, when most large battleships were decommissioned, the Navy had an Ordinance Plant and a firing range that was no longer needed. Even though the Navy was reluctant to give up the test range, there was now a Navy connection to the AEC's mission.* **On February 18, 1949, it was made official that the AEC would establish its National Reactor Testing Station (NRTS) in Idaho.**

Having chosen the site, the AEC wasted no time in breaking ground for the first reactor, the **Materials Testing Reactor,** *followed in short order by the Chemical Processing Plant, the Experimental Breeder Reactor and Navy's S1W (Submarine 1st Westinghouse reactor) Submarine Prototype Plant. The schedule urgency was such that the AEC's Field Office manager, Bill Johnson, even had the US Army assign military advisors to the NRTS to help with procurement and other tasks to maintain schedule.*

Notwithstanding the guidance of the **Reactor Safeguards Committee, politics immediately entered the site selection** *process. When it came time for KAPL to choose a site for its **first nuclear submarine prototype plant (S1G) Congressman Bill Stratton, a member of the JCAE, saw to it that it would be located in his state and in his district, at West Milton, New York.** West Milton was only a few miles from the towns of Ballston Spa and Saratoga Springs and just a little further from tri-cities of Albany, Schenectady and Troy–hardly a low population area. The prototype plant for the Combustion Engineering design was built right next to CE's facilities in Windsor, Connecticut a short 6 miles from the State's Capitol in Hartford.*

*The construction of the S1G prototype plant and the submarine to use that same reactor design, **USS Seawolf (SSN 575)** followed the same pattern as the BAPL designed nuclear propulsion plant — the prototype was scheduled to precede the submarine by about a year. However, GE's design was by far more complicated, it required materials and construction process development. **Furthermore, it used sodium, a metal that reacted exothermically if exposed to air or water. Seawolf went critical in June 1956** and operated successfully for two years. However, **a sodium fire at the prototype caused the decision to abandon that technology for naval use.** Thus, the S1G reactor was removed and Bettis S2W replaced Seawolf's reactor plant.*

*The prototype plants were an important feature of Navy's nuclear program. Their purpose was twofold: first, they were used to **test components as well the total plant system** to ensure proper operation of the design as well as later design changes, second they provided for **hands-on training and qualification of officers and enlisted men to operate Navy's nuclear fleet before their first assignment in the fleet.***

The Soviet Union was a land-based power, unlike the US which had an extensive maritime history and naval doctrine to maintain the Sea Lines of Communication (SLOCs) with other continents. The Soviet Army was the primary military force, with the Air Force and Navy providing support for the Army's defense of the USSR. Soviet missile strategy was originally centered on the land-based Strategic

Rocket Forces defending the USSR.

1963 First Soviet nuclear SSBN *Hotel* (crew 104, speed
26 kts submerged) *Dept. of Defense*

Secretary Khrushchev pushed the Soviet Navy to catch-up with the Americans and in typical Soviet fashion, nuclear submarines were turned out quickly while sacrificing safety systems. On **July 4, 1961 Soviet nuclear submarine K-19** was operating hundreds of miles north of Iceland when "...radiation detection equipment sprang to life. The reactor scrammed, shutting down...As the fuel rods climbed past one thousand degrees, the paint began burning on the reactor's outer plating...**Ivan Kulakov, a twenty-two year old chief petty officer...walked through a lake of radioactive water, ankle deep...His hands were burned as he opened valves to draw steam from the reactor...Then just as the fuel rods reached 1,470 degrees,** the pipes held, the valves held...Kulakov, whose feet and hands were irreparably burned, managed to survive with transfusions and bone marrow transplants. **He would be always crippled.** Even with all this, Moscow wasn't willing to let go of one of its few nuclear subs. **Khrushchev was still racing the Americans.**"[97]

---

[97] Sontag and Drew Op. Cit. pp. 287, 328 drawing from *"Ivan Kulakov Versus a Nuclear Reactor,"* Soviet Soldier May 1991, pp.28-31

Sergei Khrushchev (a missile engineer and son of the Soviet leader) commented that in 1962 "...It may surprise some readers that our submarine fleet, equipped with ballistic missiles, was not given as important a role at that time as US doctrine gave US *Polaris*-armed submarines....In those years we had no missiles comparable to Polaris. The range of our missiles was not half that of Polaris. Our submarines carried only **two or three missiles**, whereas US boats carried **sixteen**."[98]

In the 1960s the Soviets built-up their naval capabilities to counter US aircraft carrier battle groups and *Polaris* submarine forces. They concentrated on putting guided missiles boats aboard cruisers, submarines, and even patrol boats to threaten Navy battle groups.

Sergei Khrushchev noted, "During the previous few years submarines had become the navy's main strike force. They were grouped along both coasts of the United States. Their mission was to launch ballistic missiles against enemy cities. Submarines armed with cruise missiles lay in wait for US aircraft carriers at the outlets of harbors. They lurked not only near the coastline, but in the open ocean as well, and were capable of striking an enemy from a distance of hundreds of kilometers. The Navy's principal mission was to keep the Americans away from our shores."[99]

"ECHO II" Class

Echo II (crew 109. 22 kts submerged) launch SS-N-3A
anti-aircraft carrier cruise missile *CIA*

---

[98] Khrushchev, Op.Cit., p.470 7
[99] Khrushchev, Op.Cit. p. 468

In 1956, General Secretary Khrushchev appointed Admiral Gorshkov as Commander in Chief of the Soviet Fleet. He rapidly built-up the Soviet Navy and expanded its presence into the Mediterranean in 1968. The Soviets commissioned the **Moskva** helicopter carrier in 1967 to act as ASW command ship and developed new naval platforms and technologies. To cover and defend access to the Black Sea, the Soviet Navy deployed in the Eastern Mediterranean with a major base at Tartus Syria and several sheltered anchorages off Egypt, Libya, and Tunisia to support ships and submarines.

The USSR continued to increase its military budgets, built up its SLBM capabilities, and demonstrated their global naval reach in 1970 with over 200 ships and aviation units in the *Okean 70* exercise. In 1975, the Soviets commissioned the **Kirov** aircraft carrier, and again demonstrated their worldwide naval capabilities in the **Okean 75 exercise** involving over 200 ships, submarines, and aviation units.

USS *Johnston* (DD-821; crew 336, speed 35 kts) *US Navy*

*RADM Burnham C. "Mike" McCaffree Jr. served 40 years in the Navy from 1948-1988 through almost the entire Cold War. He recalls:

Many people know of the Soviets' efforts during the 1960s and 1970s to collect intelligence on the operations and electronic activities of U. S. Navy ships around the globe through the use of AGIs (converted fishing trawlers), Badger and Bear aircraft, and submarines. This also included trailing of our Navy aircraft carriers by AGIs and by Soviet surface combatants. Dangerously aggressive shouldering and other tactics by Soviet ships and aircraft resulted in meetings between U.S. and Soviet representatives in 1970-1972 that resulted in the **Incidents at Sea Agreement (INCSEA)** *that was signed by Secretary of the Navy John Warner and Soviet Navy Commander-in-Chief Fleet Admiral Sergey Gorshkov in mid-1972.*

The counterpoint are the U.S. intelligence collection operations from Navy patrol aircraft and submarines. My story is a tale of what happened on an occasion that involved one of our Navy's **efforts to collect intelligence on the Soviet Navy from a surface combatant.**

I was fortunate to command the GEARING class destroyer **USS JOHNSTON (DD-821)** *from 1970 to mid-1972. During the summer of 1971 we deployed with Destroyer Squadron TWO to the U. S. Sixth Fleet in the Mediterranean. A fairly significant number of combatant ships of the USSR were also deployed to the Med in what was called the* **SOVMEDRON (Soviet Mediterranean Squadron)**. *At turnover in Rota, JOHNSTON received a* **signals intelligence van that was stored in our helicopter hangar.** *It was full of communications and electronic emission intercept equipment, with a detachment of Naval Security Group technicians who would copy electronic transmissions of Soviet Navy warships that we encountered.*

In June JOHNSTON was sent on our **"sigint" mission to the eastern Med to shadow ships** *of the SOVMEDRON. One July day we were anchored east of Crete in company with most of the SOVMEDRON, including the ASW carrier LENINGRAD, a Kresta II heavy cruiser, a couple of destroyers, and an oiler. We went to General Quarters for routine training such as engineering and damage control drills and other training evolutions. Our Gunnery*

149

Officer told our forward 5" gun mounts to exercise in local control to give their pointers and trainers experience in aiming the mounts locally rather than in the normal central-control mode. Sounds like a good training idea? Yes but – guess what the forward mount's pointer and trainer aimed at? **Yep, they were aiming at the biggest "target" they could find – the LENINGRAD!**

All of a sudden, CIC called on the squawk box that our electronic warfare equipment was detecting a lot of Soviet fire control equipment being aimed at us. And then our OOD and his lookouts reported that **several of the Soviet warships had aimed their gun mounts at JOHNSTON. Next, the techies sent word that they were getting an awful lot of electronic activity and radio transmissions from the Soviet ships***. Very soon thereafter, the LENINGRAD started sending us a flashing light message from their Admiral. It said, in so many words, that we had committed a hostile act by pointing our gun mount at their ship, and they would interpret this as an ACT OF WAR if we did not immediately cease and desist. By then the Gunnery Officer had realized the cause of all the commotion –* **I suspect I "helped him" understand the problem – and the offending gun mount had been trained to centerline.**

Well, I figured that a) we were very badly outgunned by the several larger, newer Soviet warships; b) I better send a FAST apology to the Soviet Admiral; and c) hopefully the Soviets weren't interested in starting World War III by shooting up JOHNSTON. I also thought that **JOHNSTON would be getting a new CO pretty darned quick** *as soon as our Admiral (Vice Admiral "Ike" Kidd was Commander, SIXTH Fleet and he was certainly sensitive to any event that could put the U.S. in an embarrassing position in the midst of the INCSEA deliberations) got my report of what had happened. Fortunately, things calmed down – although the KRESTA cruiser chased us out of the anchorage and* **Admiral Kidd stuck up for us when the Soviet Union sent a report to Washington,** *but that was sure an exciting day for JOHNSTON. The* **PERSONAL FOR message that Admiral Kidd sent me was short and to the point and it got my attention big-time!**

*....Later, during my Amphibious Squadron TWO change of command speech I quoted that "The CO will not be able to meet his high responsible position if he does not **prepare himself and his personnel continuously and daily primarily for waging warfare**. The CO is obligated to always think about combat when he studies the combat capabilities of his ship and here weapons and equipment." And I noted that these were not words from the US Naval Institute, but this was written by **Admiral of the Soviet Fleet Gorshkov** in Morskoy Sbornik....*

*** **BURNHAM C. McCAFFREE JR.** (Mike) Rear Admiral U. S. Navy (Retired) was a Surface Warfare Officer. He was born in San Diego, CA, as the son of a career naval officer. He enlisted in the Naval Reserve in 1948, attended the Naval Academy and was commissioned an offficer in 1954. He then served in the aircraft carrier USS *Midway*, the heavy cruiser USS *Newport News*, and the destroyer USS *Gearing*. He next served as Executive Officer of the landing ship USS *Traverse County*, the landing ship dock USS *Rushmore*, and the destroyer USS *Rich*. In 1970-1972 **he commanded the destroyer USS *Johnston*, and later the amphibious transport dock USS *Shreveport* and Amphibious Squadron TWO,** conducting operations in the Atlantic Ocean and deploying to the Caribbean, Mediterranean, and Norwegian Seas and the Indian Ocean. As a junior officer he spent three years ashore in Norfolk as an ASW project officer on the Operational Test and Evaluation Force staff, and later in his career was the Torpedo Officer for the Atlantic Cruiser and Destroyer Force commander in Newport. He was the Assistant Chief of Staff (Plans) for the Commander Naval Support Activity (Danang) for one year in South Vietnam, and served in the Strategic Plans and Policy Division on the Chief of Naval Operation's staff in Washington. As a flag officer he was Director of two divisions on the CNO's staff (OPNAV), **he commanded Amphibious Group ONE in the Western Pacific and Indian Ocean, and he served as the Assistant Deputy Chief of Naval Operations (Logistics).** Since retiring from the Navy in 1988, Admiral McCaffree has been a consultant for several defense-related research companies and for the federal government. He retired in 2015 as a senior analyst for the Center for Naval Analysis (CNA).

Navy Accidents & Incidents

- September 1958 Navy P-5M crash landed in **Puget Sound; nuclear depth bomb still lost** (eventually torpedoes became more accurate that the US, Allies, and the USSR phased-out nuclear depth bombs for ASW)
- July 1961, Soviet submarine *Hotel K-19* had reactor cooling system accident
- April 1963 *USS Thresher (SSN-593)* sank with loss of crew of **129**
- December 1965, an A-4 aircraft, nuclear bomb, and pilot were lost off *USS Ticonderoga (CVA-14)* enroute to Japan; **1** killed, bomb never recovered
- July 1967 *USS Forrestal (CVA-59)* off Vietnam in Gulf of Tonkin, extensive fires and explosions, **134** lost
- February 1968 Soviet *Golf II K129* with nuclear missiles-**83** lost
- May 1968 *USS Scorpion (SSN-589)* sank in the Atlantic-**99** lost
- June 1969 *USS Frank E. Evans (DD-754)* off Vietnam, collided during the Midwatch at 0300 with the Australian carrier HMAS Melbourne (R21); **74** lost out of crew of 336 [100]
- April 1970 Soviet *November* attack submarine *K-9* sank off Spain; **52** lost
- November 1975 *USS Belknap (CG-26)* collided with *USS John F. Kennedy (CVA-67)* off Sicily; **8** lost
- August 1985 off Vladivostok, Soviet *Echo* submarine had reactor explosion; **10** killed
- October 1986 Soviet *Yankee I K-219* had missile tube explosion; **3** killed[101]

---

[100] *USS Frank E. Evans (DD-754) Association, The 74,* http://www.ussfee.org/the74.html

[101] From *List of Military Nuclear Accidents* https://en.wikipedia.org/wiki/List_of_military_nuclear_accidents

Chapter 11
The US Military Resets During the 1970s

From a high of 550,000 American troops in Vietnam in 1969 (over 3 million total were in military), **Vietnamization** efforts enabled reductions to about 24,000 troops by late 1972. While the **1973 Paris Peace Accords** temporarily "ended" the war for the US on paper, North Vietnam eventually conquered the South and the US evacuated its embassy and key personnel on April 30, 1975 to Navy ships off the coast (**Operation Frequent Wind**; I was aboard *USS Coral Sea* which along with *USS Enterprise* provided air cover for this effort. Later in May 1975, *Coral Sea* was involved in the *SS Mayaguez* operation).

The American public was tired of Vietnam and military spending; all the Service budgets shrank and the Army downsized quickly leaving thousands of combat helicopter pilots and other highly-trained specialists who had stepped-up during Vietnam suddenly having to leave the military or transition to other specialties.

The American experience in Vietnam changed forever the social dynamic of "every 18 year-old required to serve the country" and politicians quickly approved the more popular **Volunteer Military** in 1973. Today, the Selective Service website urges all men to register in case of a national emergency, citing on its front page: "Register, it's what a man has to do. It's quick, it's easy, it's the law."

My first contact with **VP** had been in 1973, when I was on a destroyer that docked at Subic Bay, Philippines. I was up at the Cubi Point BOQ and saw a very tired-looking crew checking in. I asked "Who are those guys?" and my friend said "They're a P-3 crew" and I thought, "That's what I want to be in!"

Later, aboard *USS Coral Sea*, I talked with P-3 pilots who helped and encouraged me. My boss, LCDR Steve Thiel, was instrumental in working with the XO to somehow wangle me a pilot seat in Flight School (for which I am still extremely grateful) at a time when the Navy was rapidly downsizing aviators after Vietnam.

We all remember the ***Dilbert Dunker*** (practice escape from cockpit when upside-down) *US Navy by PH2 Michael B. W. Watkins*

Flight School As it turned out, the Navy had cut too deeply and I got caught up in "PTR (Pilot Training Rate) Pushes" in both primary T-28 and advanced S-2 flight training which helped me get to a deploying P-3 squadron quickly. There have always been a number of factors including luck, timing, and ***the Needs of the Navy*** to get through Flight School. My Pre-Flight class in August 1975 was made-up of Naval Academy football players, Imperial Iranian Navy student pilots, and 5 Marine Corps artillery officers (who had been drafted (including one who hated airplanes) to be A-6 (attack jet) NFOs because they had high math scores), and several other Navy Student Naval Aviators (SNAs). We all had to pass Math, Physics, Aerodynamics, Engines and other tests--if you failed any, you had to go to Stupid Studies and pass the test before being allowed to go to Saufley Field for T-34B training. I failed Aerodynamics (which I had never taken) and so worked hard to pass and continue on.

My basic flight instructor was a fully carrier-qualified jet pilot (trained at over $1.5 million) whose class had been brought into a base theater and each given envelopes with very limited options--most were **"pink slips (Reductions In Force-RIFs)—so** he was going to school at night to become a veterinarian and was finishing a year in the Training Command.

*Retired H-46 pilot Mike Murphy remembers getting an envelope:

*"You mentioned the RIFs in Flight School; in the **Summer of 1970 I was one of those guys called into the auditorium and told that there were too many of us and not enough instructors or airplanes,** so some of us had to be released. Added to that, the prop pipeline had been shut down due to a hurricane that hit NAS Corpus. We were each given an envelope with a slip of paper that either said "You have been retained" or "You have been released." My understanding was that they released the bottom 50% of the class and anyone who had a "Down" (failed flight).*

***They released about 450 guys from Pensacola Florida area bases who walked out of the auditorium and out of flight school that day.** Everyone retained was told they would be helicopter pilots. Those released could go by Air Force and Marines tables; Air Force took about 200 guys and Marines took about 50. I like to think that the forced induction of the top graded students from flight school that year had a lasting impact on the helicopter community.*

***After the RIF I went to Ellison Field where we were pushed through quickly, but by the time I got my wings in December 1970 it was time to wait again.** The HAL-3 (combat Vietnam helicopters) pipeline had opened and closed several times and I missed the window. The Helo RAGs were full, so I had to wait about a year and a half at NAS Alameda where I flew H-34s, Hueys, U-11s, S-2s, and C-1s—great experience and a lot of fun. I was waiting for a slot in LAMPS (light helos deployed on destroyers)... but, I met a couple of guys from the H-46 (large two-rotor helos)* *community and they talked me into becoming one of the last **"Rodeo Pilots" doing VERTREP** (Vertical Replenishment) for ships in the fleet"*

UNREP, H-46 on USS Mars (AFS-1) *Michael Cowan photo*

***Mike Murphy served 23 years active duty in the Navy. He was a merchant maritime academy graduate and had sailed commercially before activating his Navy commission to go to flight school. Mike did three squadron tours, including command of HC-11, and two tours on LPHs (large Landing Pad Helicopter carriers,) where he not only got to fly, but also to use his ship driving skills. Mike retired out of the OPNAV Staff in Washington DC as an O-6 in 1992 and was hired by a commercial shipping company where he sailed for another 16 years as a Captain on commercially operated government ships. From 2008 until present Mike Murphy has been the Vice President for Government Relations in Washington representing the American Maritime Officers union's interests to the U.S. government, Congress and at the International Maritime Organization in London.

The T-28C was a very sturdy military aircraft fielded in 1949; during flight school we were also trained on other post-WWII generation Navy aircraft--the T-34B and the S-2A. We learned a lot in a short time at Whiting Field (built by German POWs in WWII) in VT-3, which was the primary squadron dedicated to training future

"Multi-engine" pilots. During preflight, you wanted to see some oil- -but not too much—leaking from the big 1820 cubic inch engine used on many aircraft, including the WWII B-17. **(Tom Landry , Gene Rodenberry, Smokey Yunnick, and Jimmy Stewart flew the B-17, Tennessee Ernie Ford was a B-17 Bombardier, Clark Gable was a gunner/ photographer, and Norman Lear was a radio operator).**

You sat up high, strapped in behind a big **radial R-1820 engine putting out around 1500 HP with a reassuring solid pulsing of the 9 cylinders combined with the heat oil, AVGAS smells, and busy radio traffic provided a great training experience.** On takeoff, you put in a lot of right rudder to counter *P-factor* (asymmetric blade, disc effect); constantly kept your outside scan going, and were always ready to do an engine failure or practice PEL (Precautionary Emergency Landing) if the instructor threw one at you.

One day as we were climbing out, I had gone through the After-Takeoff procedure of closing the canopy, setting props-throttles-mixtures, etc., when an unusually friendly instructor inquired where I was from. I said "from a farm in Upstate New York" and he asked what we raised there and I was saying corn and alfalfa when **he screamed, "Do you ever raise any gear?"** --I put the gear up fast and never forgot that again.

One of our student friends at NAS Whiting had a night engine failure and was able to put the T-28 into a field and later, out of NAS Corpus Christi, a twin-engine **S-2A** had a complete electrical failure at night and the instructor/ student bellied into a field. Mechanics soon hammered out the dents in the fuselage, hung new props, and the Grumman *"Iron Works"* S-2A flew again.

Learning to fly the T-28 in formation was big step; I remember our night formation flight with the "Fam Space" instructor keeping an eye on 3 of us as we flew a triangular course over West Florida and South Alabama. During this period, we SNAs (Student Naval Aviators) started feeling we were learning more very fast a la the firehouse method; you didn't think about it you just did it. As of the PTR push I was flying 3-4 flights a day and one day up at Brewton (Alabama), my instructor kept telling me to "stay on altitude 1200 feet," and I said "I am on 1200 feet," but I wasn't—I was so tired I was fixating on 1200 on the RPM gauge. On the 3-day 1976 Presidents' weekend holiday, about 5 of us were told to "finish ground school" and we cleaned-up all our courses so we could drive down to Corpus Christi for Advanced Prop training in the S-2A. We had to do a final cross country and we got to fly from Corpus to El Toro MCAS in Tustin California. On the way back at night, we stopped for gas at Davis Monthan AFB in Tucson and ground control taxied us for a long time—we asked again where the gas was—and they said **"Gas? We have newer S-2s than yours in "the Bone Yard" and so we were sending you there!**

1976 was the United States Bicentennial Year; I received my Navy wings (we owed the Navy 4 ½ years after getting wings) in June and checked into VP-30 at NAS Jacksonville for 5+ months of ASW tactics and flight training in the P-3C before joining VP-45 around Christmas as the squadron deployed to KEF for a 5+ month deployment. This was about 18 months after I came off a 7-month *WestPac* cruise as an Officer of the Deck (Fleet) on *USS Coral Sea CVA-43)*. During this deployment, Vietnam fell and *Coral Sea* was involved in covering the evacuation of Saigon and the *SS Mayaguez* rescue operation.

Chapter 12
U.S. Patrol Aircraft Evolution

P-2 *Neptune* rigging *Moskva* Helicopter ASW carrier *US Navy*

Navy VP squadrons' mission is **long-range patrol support for the Fleet** at sea by providing anti-submarine, surveillance, and intelligence capabilities. During the 1950s and 1960s the US Navy transitioned its long-range patrol mission from flying boats, airships, and Lockheed P-2V *Neptunes* to the P-3A *Orion* which was a modified commercial Lockheed *Electra* L-188.

Patrol Squadron Reservists were an integral part of the Navy

*TACCO/ PPTN (TacNav) / RIO John McMahon CDR USNR (Ret.) recalls his career in 3 Services:

*I enlisted as a **USMC PFC Reservist** when I was a junior in high school in Connecticut. After graduating from college in*

Montana, I completed **USAF Navigator and Radar Intercept Officer (RIO)** training in **1962**, then accumulated 500 hours as an RIO in the back seat of **F-89J Scorpions** for the **Montana and Oregon Air National Guard (ANG) squadrons from late 1962 to early 1966.** The F-89J was one of the primary Air Defense Command **all-weather interceptors** during the early-1950's to early-1960's, and its **mission was to identify any unknown aircraft penetrating the U. S. ADIZ (Air Defense Identification Zone)** and carry **two MB-1 nuclear air-to-air rockets** to counter the Soviet inter-continental bomber threat.

In early 1966 my Oregon ANG squadron converted from **F-89J's to the F-102 Delta Dart single seat interceptor, so I lost my RIO billet.** I then **inter-service transferred to the Naval Air Reserve at NAS Seattle** where several Reserve patrol squadrons were flying the SP-2E, to be replaced by the SP-2H in 1967. I gained a **USN navigator designator (1325)**, and flew in the Neptunes from July 1966 to Sept 1975, as navigator, PPTN, and TACCO, ending up with 852 hours in the SP-2E/H type. During that time our annual cruises took us to NAS Barbers Point, NAS Jacksonville, NAS Los Alamitos, NAS Willow Grove, and Rota, Spain, where I had the memorable experiences of **both flying in the Med observing Soviet naval vessel movements and navigating the return of an SP-2H from Rota (Spain) to NAS South Weymouth via the Azores, Labrador and Nova Scotia.**

In 1970 the Seattle SP-2H squadrons moved to NAS Whidbey Island. At about the same time the smaller reserve squadrons were consolidated and reformed as **VP-69, of which I am a plank owner (original member).** We flew the SP2-H's from Whidbey until late 1975 when we began the transition to the **P-3A Orion.** From January 1976 until July 1978 I flew as a **TacNav (PPTN)** in the P-3, until I was promoted to Commander and lost my VP-69 squadron billet. During that time, I accumulated 259 hours in the P-3, with annual cruises to NAS Barbers Point and my final memorable cruise to Guam. After spending my final year with the NAS Whidbey PATWING, I retired with 21 good years of Reserve service, and am **proud to have worn the uniforms of** *three branches of the U. S. military service* during that time, *thoroughly enjoying my time with each.*

Box Lunches:

*John McMahon remembers: We old P-2 folks remember well that the box lunch was an essential piece of gear on those long overwater P2 flights. However, procuring the box lunches before a flight was one of the least favorite duties that often befell the crew's Navigator, and one of the tasks that made one **question whether USN Patrol Plane aviation had really made it into the jet age.**

In addition to gathering up the Nav bag, ONC charts, sextant, weighted code book and Tac Aid bag, the PPTN was often the one who had to collect $1.10 from each crew member, find his way to the galley at zero dark thirty at some strange NAS, then pay cash for and gather up the box lunches before proceeding to the flight line in time for taxi and takeoff. *After having done that, I think that I enjoyed my box lunch more, especially the cold fried chicken, because I often had some extra effort invested in it.* **But, it always drove me crazy that the USN galley and NAS ops system had to use such an antiquated system to provide its intrepid air crews with a simple $1.10 box lunch.**

...For the first few years (it wasn't box lunches from the galley to the flight line), **just my brown sack lunch and thermos bottle,** *often enjoyed standing up under the canopy of a big Douglas fir or cedar with the rain or snow falling, and sometimes with the sun shining and the breeze blowing, but* **always much quieter than when sitting between those two big radial engines on the P-2.**

*P-2 Patrol Plane Commander Roger Stambaugh recalls how "Some Navs owed me big time!"

My summer job in 1967 was at Andrews AFB between semesters in dental school (multiple series of drills and several two-week duty assignments). I was to take various squadrons (none of *them mine) on their two week "excursion". I joined an unnamed squadron at their NAS. On a flight from Shearwater Nova Scotia to Rota Spain, about two hours out, the **Nav said he was lost and I had it.** He was giving up. **I always carried a two-sided chart of the Atlantic in my flight suit. The Atlantic is after all a lake compared to the Pacific. I dialed-in the Azores commercial radio station on the ADF, knowing that there was a duty free across the street from operations.** We made it to Rota well prepared for the two weeks of duty. How one can become **lost in the Atlantic** is beyond me.*

*(With my magic Lockheed-provided **"lode stone"** in the panel, a watch, the Chevron gas station equivalent of an airborne road map of the Atlantic and wind on the water, a P-2 driver could go anywhere. (You'd rarely see a P-2 above the cloud cover) No new-fangled gadgets like a sextant needed!)*

*(....and don't forget all the gallons of coffee passed forward **over the wing beam on the P-2***)

***Roger Stambaugh: "I took my written and physicals for the NAVCAD (Naval Aviation Cadet) program at NAS Sandpoint in 1957, joined NAVCAD class 10-58, and received my **wings in November 1959. After survival, JJ, and nuclear delivery and loading schools at NAS North Island, I joined VP19 at NAS Alameda** in December 1959. VP19 deployed to Kodiak that Spring and we flew the usual flights way, way west of Shimya. I qualified as PPC in 1961. In 1963 I joined the Reserve P-2 squadron at NAS Sandpoint (Seattle) and in 1965 transferred to the Reserve P-2 squadron at Andrews AFB. I rejoined the NAS Sandpoint P-2 squadron in October 1969 and qualified as PPC, NATOPS and Instrument Check Pilot. We relocated the squadron to NAS Whidbey in, as I recall, 1970. I am a **Plank Owner (original member) in VP-69**. I completed my career at NAS Point Magu as a PPC in P-2's (over 3,000 hours in P-2's) and later as **Commanding Officer of ASW 6019. I taught wargaming part-time (1975-1978) at the Naval War College** until I retired as a Commander in 1980; I retired as a periodontist and am now living in Washington State."

In 1959-60, several fatal airline *Electra* crashes had given it a reputation as a deadly airplane since some wings had failed due to weak engine mounts and harmonic metal fatigue. In 1959 the Navy contracted with Lockheed to develop the P-3A based on the *Electra* and the P-3A became operational in 1962. The last P-3 was produced in 1990 and has now been replaced by the Boeing P-8 *Poseidon*.

The Navy heavily modified the *Electra* by taking 7 feet out of the fuselage, strengthening and stiffening the wing, strengthening engine mounts, adding weapons hardpoints, a "synchrophaser" for the propellers, a bomb bay, and all the ASW equipment/antennas including a MAD (Magnetic Anomaly Detector) boom on the tail. The result was the powerful P-3A (and later the -B, -C, and Updates II, II.5, and III) which was a reliable fuel-efficient performer at low altitudes and could loiter on 2 or 3 powerful engines to fly 8 to 11-hour missions.

The P-3C was the Navy's first computerized patrol aircraft; in the 1970s it cost about $37M and was one of the most expensive aircraft in the Navy inventory. It had taken a decade of dedicated work by leading engineers in the Navy and industry to develop it into an effective long-range patrol platform to support the Fleet in taking on the growing Soviet submarine threat.

The P-3C had a max gross weight of 139,760 pounds and was powered by four Allison T-56-14As each capable of developing 4600 shaft horse power. The P-3Cs fuel flow was about 4500 lbs. per hour, with cruise at 330 knots True Air Speed, and a range of about 2400 nautical miles.

The first time I pushed the power levers forward and **called "Takeoff Horsepower" to the Flight Engineer, I was impressed by how quickly the turboprops came up and pushed you back in the seat**---you knew that this plane had plenty of extra power and would be a rugged and dependable workhorse...and it had the very latest computer technology!

In the early 1970s, the US Navy transitioned from years of deploying ships and aircraft for Vietnam duties toward more traditional battle groups and rebuilding the Fleets' Anti-Submarine Warfare (ASW) mission.

Joe Brundage LCDR USN (Ret.)

*LCDR Joe Brundage enlisted in the Navy in 1970 and remembers his career:

*"It was nice to go the VP-45 Reunion and just be with old friends and comrades; it brought back a lot of memories from my 26 years in Naval Aviation. I started out in the early Seventies at NAS Dallas in VF-201 and **F-8 Crusaders**. I was the night check line supervisor and had too many 16-hour shifts. Management in the squadron was frustrating. We worked too many 7-day weeks and the poor people walked around tired like zombies. I am surprised no one got hurt on the flight deck. We were deployed aboard USS John F. Kennedy (CVA-67) and I was a plane captain in an F-8, when one night my plane was about 6 inches from getting pushed over the side.*

*Frustrated, I put in a dream sheet for several VR & VP squadrons. One day they said you need to go to Admin, your orders to **VP-67 at Memphis** came in. I thought they were kidding and ignored them until the Admin Chief came to the line shack. So, I happily transferred to the VP squadron.*

You know how they'll try to razz you at a new unit. Well, they told me to go drop the chin cowl on a P-2V engine. (It was armor plated.) When I unlatched the last latch, it knocked me down, to a peal of laughter; the **R-3350 cowls were armor-plated. The fuel cell bladders were self-sealing. The cockpit floor was armored.** *It was a tough old bird.*

Then I found out I could be a Flight Crew Plane Captain which is what they called a **Flight Engineer (F/E)** *on the P-2. We took off with helmets on, and you could only talk on Intercom System (ICS) as the recips (18-cylinder reciprocating engines) were so loud.*

I then had a Private Pilot's License and was working on a Commercial license. I was also the only single F/E. So, I got a lot of cross countries and stick time. The P-2 did not have an auto pilot. It did have altitude hold with control wheel steering. It trimmed up well. One weekend we went to the Air Force base at Navato CA, north of the Golden Gate. Coming back, the co-pilot, who was badly hung over, wanted to be relieved to go get oxygen. **The plane commander slapped me on the knee and put me in the left seat. He had sunglasses on, so I thought he was watching me. I basically flew from San Francisco to Albuquerque.** *I had the flight plan and a grease pencil. When Center called, I'd write the new freq(uency) on the side glass and change freqs. I changed the VOR/TACAN, dialed in the new course. Climbed when they told me to climb, re-leaned the engines. Then entered IMC and flew on. At Albuquerque the* **plane commander suddenly jerked awake and shouted, where are we?** *He had been* **asleep** *for I don't know how long. I showed him on the Low Alt IFR chart as we were IMC and he said my airplane skills were good.*

There was another F/E who told me **this one Reservist let him land the plane.** *So, I flew with him and asked; he put me in the left seat. The P-2 had a huge single main mount. It had a 15:1 glide ratio. It was actually a little hard to get it down when light. It would float in ground affect if you were a smidgen fast. A good hand could touch down so lightly, you couldn't feel it. There was* *a **prop-reverse override switch**, my job to hold onto it-- so you could go into reverse instead of waiting to get the weight on gear switch to complete the circuit and go into reverse.*

*The P-2 may not have been fast, but leaned-out engines and bomb bay fuel bladders gave it **16+ hours endurance.** It also bordered on cruel and unusual punishment. I remember looking for a sub around Midway. We were having trouble getting triangulation with sonobouys until the AO saw the periscope and came up in the cockpit. Apparently, there was an ICS recorder, and we were told not to talk on the ICS if we saw a visual, so the ASWOC would give us credit for a find with sonobouys. So, the AW made-up data and we went over to the periscope and dropped more bouys and got credit for a find. We followed him for 2-3+ days. One plane going on station, one on station, one coming back. We maintained hot turnovers. The P-2 only had a Sensor 1; no Sensor 2. An AT manned the Radar, etc.*

Then I went to P-3s and it was like moving from a beat-up ranch pickup into a Cadillac. *Quiet, pressurized and air-conditioned; a real upgrade.* ***The P-2 and P-3 LCDRs (Lieutenant Commanders) of the 1970s that I flew with were of a different breed. They were gents and knew their stuff. They made sure the enlisted were berthed and taken care of. VP-45 in the 1980s was different.*** *I was also in another VP squadron--where some folks had big chips on their shoulders. It was so odd; Generational shift, I guess.*

***Joe Brundage LCDR USN (Ret.) grew up in the Atlanta GA area and enlisted in the Navy in January 1970 and went to Aviation Structural Mechanic Hydraulics (AMH) "A" school. He was assigned to VF-201 (F-8 Crusaders) and went aboard the USS John F. Kennedy (CVA-67), then to VP-67 NAS Memphis, VR-54 NAS Atlanta, and VP-68 NAS Patuxent River and VP-62 NAS JAX, where he finished a BS degree. He flew as a flight engineer on C-118Bs, P-2Vs & P-3s. He was selected and frocked to CPO; then went to AOCS in Pensacola and was commissioned in September 1980 and became an Aerospace Maintenance Duty Officer. He served as Maintenance Control Officer in VP-45, as AIMD Avionics/Armament Division Officer at NAS JAX, and Assistant Maintenance Officer on board USS Carl Vinson (CVN-70). He then served as Assistant Maintenance Officer VX-5 China Lake where he earned an MS degree, then served as OIC Medium Attack Weapons Det. NAF El Centro (A-6 Intruders), and lastly as Wing Maintenance Officer at Fleet Logistics Support Wing at NAS Dallas. Joe retired to Colorado to take care of his parents, became a rancher, and flies his Cessna 195 tail-dragger.

Chapter 13
Hunting Soviet Submarines on a P-3C Crew Out of Keflavik (KEF) Iceland

"On Top" Soviet sub pipes (periscope, EW mast) *US Navy*

Background Late 1970s-early 1980s

During the late 1970s our squadron VP-45 deployed to Keflavik (KEF) Iceland and twice to Sigonella Sicily for 6-month deployments against Soviet Navy submarines. Decreasing real military spending affected the Navy and some ASW readiness slipped. During this timeframe, Soviet Mig-25 fighter interceptor pilot **Victor Belenko defected** to Japan, the Arabs embargoed oil to the US, and NATO agreed to install over 500 short and medium-range nuclear missiles in Western Europe. President Carter negotiated the Camp David Accords, the Panama Canal Treaty, and normalized relations with Red China. In 1979 he faced the Iran Hostage Crisis, the second world oil "shock" (due to interruptions of Iranian oil), and the Soviet invasion of Afghanistan which **ended *Détente*** and carrying out the recent ***SALT II agreement.***

Admiral Stansfield Turner, the Director of the CIA under President Carter, led its "...covert actions aimed at Moscow, Warsaw, and Prague, printing and distributing magazines and journals to Poland and Czechoslovakia, **circulating the written work of dissidents in the Soviet Union, placing fax machines and tape cassettes in the hands of people behind the Iron Curtain**. These acts approved by Mr. Carter and his National Security Adviser, Zbigniew Brzezinski, sought to subvert the control of information which was the foundation in the Communist world."

Director Turner recalled that "We were appreciating as early as '78 that the Soviet economy was in serious trouble...(but) we didn't make the leap that we should have made—I should have made—**that the economic trouble would lead to political trouble**. We thought they would tighten their belt under a Stalin-like regime and continue marching on."[102]

Terrorist threats increased during the late 1970s to early 1980s and the American military personnel and their families were vulnerable. In 1972 Palestinian terrorists struck at the 1972 Munich Olympics; in 1970s Germany- Red Army Faction-Bader-Meinhoff Gang was active; 1978 Italy-the Red Brigade killed former Prime Minister Moro and kidnapped US Army General Dozier in 1981. In 1982 Beirut, Lebanon truck bombs killed over 300 American and French military; and 1986 FB-111 reprisal strikes on Benghazi Libya for its role in the La Belle Discotheque bombing which killed 4 and injured over 200.

In 1977 during President Carter's Administration, leading conservative critics who believed that the Soviet Union was gaining nuclear supremacy formed the ***Committee on the Present Danger.*** Paul Nitze and Eugene Rostow co-chaired the committee and members included 33 future Reagan Administration officials

---

[102] Tim Weiner, Obituary *Stansfield Turner, Selected by Carter to Lead a Battered CIA, Dies at 94, The New York Times,* January 20, 2018, p. B14

such as George Shultz who became Secretary of State and John Lehman who became Secretary of the Navy.

In 1979 President Carter and Premier Brezhnev signed the **Salt II Treaty which limited each power to 1200 ICBMs and 1200 SLBMs, a maximum of 10 Multiple Independent Reentry Vehicles (MIRV) warheads per missile, and limits on missile development including Intermediate-Range Nuclear Forces.** SALT II was never ratified by the Senate and diplomacy was scuttled by the 1979 Soviet invasion of Afghanistan.

Both superpowers continued to build-up their conventional and nuclear military capabilities. The Soviets rapidly expanded their nuclear delivery systems--including submarines--and exceeded the US in nuclear "throw weight" capabilities. The *New York Times* reported in late 1977 that the Soviets had built a massive new missile submarine named **Typhoon** to rival our upcoming **Trident** boats. The *Typhoon* was massive (563 feet long with 20 ballistic missiles) and by 1980 the Soviet Navy had 94 cruise and ballistic missile boats and 71 attack boats.

The United States' ability to survive a **first strike**, capability to conduct a **second strike**, and whether a nuclear war could be *"won"* were debated vigorously. John Newman observed that "If taken seriously, **the first strike threat applied with greater threat to the Soviet Union; roughly 75 percent** of its strategic weapons were deployed in vulnerable silos, as distinct from **just 25 percent of the American forces**—a more balanced mix of ICBMs, SLBMs, and heavy bombers...The side attacked could empty its silos if forewarned or use its surviving weapons to destroy the other. But common sense was no match for the minatory bolt from the blue; it had become the fashionable anxiety...So does the corollary preposition (to powers deploying nuclear arms) **that a nuclear war can be won**. Even with a large enough second-strike capacity to destroy the Soviet Union many times over, *American policy was captive in the 1970s and most of the 1980s—and to a degree still is— to the Pearl Harbor psychology: **by fear of a bolt from the blue.**"[103]

In the early 1980s, **President Reagan** embarked on a large defense build-up, including more aggressive military operations,

---

[103] Newhouse, Op. Cit., pp. 298, 426

growth toward a **600 ship Navy**, and the massive **"Star Wars"** missile defense shield technologies program. The Soviets worried that Star Wars (combined with the short and intermediate missiles stationed in Europe) "...would upset the delicate balance of nuclear deterrence that had governed the entire nuclear age. **Mutually Assured Destruction** had kept crises from slipping into hot war for more than a generation. So long as each superpower retained the ability to annihilate the other, the theory ran, neither would ever dare to attack. Perhaps no longer." [104]

The new *Trident* **D5 SLBMs** provided such increased accuracy combined with stealth and mobility, that the Soviets feared a potential "decapitation strike" by the US which motivated them to create "Systema Perimetr" or the **"Dead Hand"** nuclear control system to enable a Second Strike-back capability. [105]

Admiral James Watkins, a submariner and Chief of Naval Operations put it this way "The mission of the strategic deterrent at sea is not first strike. It is called war termination strategy...**So the first strike was inter continental ballistic missiles, obviously, The land-based missiles were the most destabilizing of the elements of the deterrent.** The maritime forces, while they were **large in numbers of warheads, were there for the war termination strategy, which said "How do you win such a thing?...But who wins the battle is going to be largely a function of how much you have left after the first exchange**...that's the reality of when you get into offensive weaponry on both sides as a strategic deterrent as opposed to strategic defense...These (submarine launched ballistic missiles) were the backup forces necessary to—you might say—to undergird a nuclear exchange, and our job, of course, was to **set up a deterrent that would make it unwise to do that, and we did it. And I believe it is one of the reasons we were able to bring the Russians to their knees in the cold war.**"[106]

---

[104] Engel J., *When the World Seemed New; George H.W. Bush and the End of the Cold War,* Houghton Mifflin Harcourt Publishing Co., New York 2017, pp.15-16

[105] *Dead Hand,* Wiki https://en.wikipedia.org/wiki/Dead_Hand_(nuclear_war)

[106] Sontag and Drew, Op. Cit., pp 323-324

Greenland-Iceland-United Kingdom (GIUK) Gap

Greenland-Iceland-UK (GIUK) Gap *CIA*

Deploying to KEF We lugged our gear into Hangar 1000 of Naval Air Station (NAS) JAX(sonville) around Christmas 1976 for VP-45s five to six-month deployment to Keflavik, Iceland. 23 of us boarded a P-3C and I squeezed into my assigned spot which was **a fold-down seat sandwiched between two computer equipment bays.** It had taken me 18 intense months at flight school and VP-30 RAG (Replacement Air Group) learning the P-3 and ASW tactics to get into this seat and I was very glad—and apprehensive--about finally joining a deploying operational patrol squadron to fly the new P-3C. Today, I am still amazed by how the squadron could expeditiously pack-up all its gear into collapsible metal footlockers, load aboard 3 Air Force C-141s, fly 9 P-3Cs, and deploy far away to start immediate ASW operations.

We had left the live oaks, humidity, and morning paper mill smell of JAX for cold and windy Keflavik on the Arctic Circle, where in late December there were only 4-5 hours of sun hanging low on the horizon. We landed at KEF in blustery darkness, were towed into the old WWII hangar, and the main cabin door opened and in came the cold air, Icelandic Customs officers, and our squadron mates.

Our sister squadron VP-49 was in the process of turning over to VP-45 and our arriving crews immediately were put on rest and went on the schedule for operational patrols ASAP. As an incoming 45 crew went out on an 8-hour patrol relieving a 49 crew and silently (we were always in EMCON--Emissions Control) picking up submarine contact, a 49 crew was released to return to JAX.

Soviet Yankee II (crew 120, 27kts submerged) missile boat *US Navy*

The KEF routine was go to briefing, fly 8-hour mission, debrief, go to *Brass Nut*, sleep (sometimes not much), try to do ground job at hangar...and repeat. I showed up with my crew at our first mission brief and a senior LT asked **"Who the f_ are you? Let's see some ID"** since I did look strange as a brand-new junior pilot wearing LT bars, fresh from the RAG.

While the *Brass Nut* was just a BOQ room converted to a bar run by the Ready 2 crew who stocked it and kept it in a constant state of readiness for visitors, the *'Nut* provided a very important international hub for camaraderie among ASW crews and visitors. If you got there after hours, the crew would tend its own bar; we always stopped by the *'Nut* to "debrief" after every mission. I have heard from several sources that apparently this "debrief" tradition slowed-down in later years as flyers became more self-contained and less crew-focused.

> *One morning about 0730 we walked out of the 'Nut with beer bottles in hand and a little kid standing at a school bus stop in the dark pointed at me and asked his Mom* **"Why is that pilot drinking beer in the morning?"** *as she quickly hustled him onto the bus and away from our bad influence.*

We hosted Canadian, British, Dutch, and any other crews who might be coming through KEF at the Brass Nut. The *'Nut* and Chief Petty Officers *"Saloon," First Class'* mess: *"the Coon Saloon,"* and *Acey-Duecy* clubs were essential as KEF was so isolated in the North Atlantic. For an idea of *'Nut* creativity, here is a recipe posted by a 1980s RAF *Nimrod* officer on the British PPRuNE website:

> *"...from that classy establishment, the Brass Nut on NAS Keflavik: the "Upside down Margarita on the bar:" Sitting on a bar stool, back to the bar, head lying on the bar top, mouth open; barman pours all the ingredients of the margarita directly into your mouth. Close mouth, sit up, shake head to mix ingredients—down in one. Oh the cultural joys of Iceland in the winter time when it's Chill Index 4 and you're not allowed outside. NOT!! The Ancient Mariner"*[107]

---

[107] *The Ancient Mariner* 2015, British *PPRuNE Professional Pilots Rumor Network* website, www.pprune.org

USS Skipjack (SSN-585; crew 93, >31 kts submerged*) "No Slack in Fast Attack"* US Navy *All Hands* magazine July 1965 (my cousin was a Reactorman on this boat)

*Admiral James Stavridis, former NATO commander and a Surface Warfare Officer, observed;

*"What was cold war like in the Atlantic? First and foremost, it was a battle for control—really complete surveillance and the positioning of strategic and tactical assets—in the Greenland-Iceland-United Kingdom (GIUK) gap...This zone of thousands of miles of empty ocean became critical strategically...Thus in the cold war, there was a constant maneuver between the Soviet Union (and its Warsaw Pact allies) and the NATO forces led by the United States for the control of the (GIUK) gap. This required significant deployments of US combat power to Iceland, Canada, Denmark, and of course the United Kingdom itself. Combat power was also stationed at base in the Northeast. The operative maritime forces were **long-range P-3 Orion anti-submarine warfare aircraft,** formidable hunter-killer machines used to find*

*Soviet submarines; **nuclear attack submarines** of the United States and our allies; satellite coverage of the deep ocean; and occasional deployments of **destroyers and cruisers** (like mine) with significant sonar, torpedo, and other sensors suitable to pursue submarines. The Soviets deployed their ballistic missile submarines (equipped with long-range missiles tipped with nuclear weapons) as well of flotillas of submarines and surface ships. While not exactly crowded up there, it was a "target rich zone" for antisubmarine forces."* [108]

Cold War sub-hunting was very complex and expensive, requiring extensive coordination between Submarine, Surface, and Air and our Allies' ASW platforms which all contributed to round-the-clock tracking of submarines. VP provided unique long-range and rapid reaction capabilities to support the Navy Fleet ASW and intelligence gathering. During the Cold War, the East Coast Navy deployed VP squadrons continuously to Keflavik, Bermuda, Lajes Azores, Rota Spain, and Sigonella Sicily. Norway, UK, Canada, and the Netherlands all contributed patrol aircraft-- and often worked together out of KEF and other bases.

Norwegian P-3s initially tracked Russian subs as they transited around the Kola Peninsula and turned them over to US P-3s. Our mission was to locate and/or track the subs (missile or attack) as they proceeded south to determine whether they were heading toward the **GIUK gaps**: G-I gap (Greenland-Iceland) which meant they were headed deep into the Atlantic or via the I-UK gap (Iceland-United Kingdom) to head down towards the eastern Atlantic or possibly by Gibraltar into the Mediterranean.

VP squadrons were focused on tracking Russian missile boats which were a key strategic threat to the US. In 1977, the Soviets had about 33 *Yankee* missile boats (1300-mile missile range) and 21 newer *Delta* boats (their 4200-mile range meant they didn't even have to go to sea to reach US targets.) The **Yankees had to operate relatively close in patrol areas east of Bermuda and in the Eastern Pacific** to target US cities and defense establishments with nuclear ballistic missiles.

---

[108] Stavridis, Op. Cit., pp. 82-83

While American submarines were the premier anti-submarine force; VP's job was to locate and track submarines and be ready in the event of a nuclear war, to assist in attacking Soviet *"boomers"* before they launched their ICBMs or to torpedo Soviet attack boats threatening our submarines. During our KEF deployment, the Soviet Northern Fleet--comprised of about 125 submarines--conducted its annual month-long exercise which NATO named *SpringEx 77.*

Tragically, throughout these times, a US Navy spy ring led by retired Submariner John Walker, his son, and Jerry Whitworth (retired radioman) were very active in providing highly-classified information to the Soviets. Although we didn't know about them then, **many of our ASW efforts were being compromised** due to their greed for money--not ideology. According to Sontag and Drew "...the Soviets had been listening in on US communications, and **without the years of research, investment in technology, or risk to men's lives.** In fact, **Walker's ring had cost the Soviets less than $1 million over eighteen years, and for that money he had almost single-handedly destroyed the US nuclear advantage."**[109]

*TACCO Warren Tisdale remembers checking into the VP-45 in Winter 1977 at Keflavik Iceland:

*"Steve F.... picked me up in the duty truck when I got off the Air Force C-141 transport at Keflavik; he said the squadron was in a **FLAP. I may have missed the term while training in VP-30, so Frick explained it stood for 'F...ing Launch All Planes.'** It was not unusual to be in contact with a Soviet submarine on the flights out of Keflavik; the water seemed to be good for propagating sound. On my first mission, we happened to see a Soviet Bear (TU-95 bomber) transiting south, and we tracked a submarine. My Plane Commander made a big deal out of my getting two Soviet contacts on my first flight. One nice thing about KEF was the relatively long transit (compared to SIG) back to base—plenty of time for paperwork."*

---

[109] Sontag and Drew, Op. Cit., p.249

VP-45 P-3C (crew 12, range 2400nm at 328 kts) over Iceland *US Navy*

Crew Concept The squadron had 12 Combat Air Crews (CACs). Each crew contained 12 men (5 officers and 7 enlisted): 2 NFOs--TACCO and a NAVCOM, 3 pilots (Patrol Plane Commander-PPC, Second Pilot-2P, and 3P), a Flight Engineer and a Second Mech(anic), 2 Acoustic and 1 Non-acoustic sensor operators, an Ordnanceman, and an IFT (In Flight Technician).

What really counted was your ability to work smoothly within a team and contribute to the crew's success. For pilots, it was very important to gain the trust of the crew and not scare them by taking risks or throwing the plane around—and hard landings did not help. I immediately liked the VP crew concept because everyone was recognized primarily by their professional abilities- and we worked to weld ourselves into a close team.

New NFOs and pilots were integrated into crews, continuously trained, and watched closely to prepare them for increased responsibility. Both Naval Flight Officers (NFOs) and pilots could become Mission Commanders and attain squadron command. The average squadron tour was 3 years, so **every year between deployments, 1/3 of crewmembers and squadron personnel**

were replaced, which meant that we were constantly studying and training to upgrade quickly to rebuild crew qualifications in preparation for the next deployment.

The crew I was assigned to for 3 years was a constantly changing composite of varying backgrounds as new members rotated in: we were a cross-section from many backgrounds; **most of us were from small inland towns** looking for adventure and to fly to serve our country. Some of us had come through Navy ROTC or the Naval Academy and others off the street via AOCS (Aviation Officer Candidate School).

Crews were briefed 3 hours ahead of takeoff time and then were dropped off to preflight the aircraft. We dropped our gear and helmet (to be worn in case of ditching) bags near our stations and started our routines. As the crew's junior pilot, my job was to preflight the outside of the aircraft and I remember KEFs cold darkness, the gusting, trying to do a good preflight with my flashlight, and wanting to get back into the cozy warmth of the plane.

During preflight, if any of the critical ASW avionics or mechanical systems went hard down, everyone had to pack-up their gear and move quickly over to another aircraft and work to make-up lost time in order make the assigned takeoff time. **Everything was built around getting on station exactly on time to relieve an on-station crew passively** and conduct a smooth turnover on a hopefully hot contact. It took about 2 hours to get out on station with 4 hours on station, and then 2 hours back home. I was extremely impressed by entire squadron's determination and total focus on its mission of prosecuting Soviet submarines aggressively and maintaining passive sonobuoy contact.

While some crews just seemed lucky and were more successful at finding and hanging onto subs, luck was only a small part--**it was really all about creating a team and meshing together crewmembers' skills and personalities to make them a smooth-functioning crew.** We trained, flew, and went everywhere together—especially on deployment.

Enlisted and officers took tests to qualify for flying positions. You had to make it through the training (getting good instructors helped), have the grades, and timing to get into an operational squadron and a good crew. The Navy continuously adjusted the aviation training pipeline according to its needs and was quick to adjust or close it.

Squadrons Each squadron developed a different personality and reputation depending on a combination of its leadership, personnel, and history. A squadron had 350-400 personnel including crews and hundreds of very skilled sailors in trades ranging from mechanics and avionics technicians to operational and tactical support for our 9 ASW aircraft. There were 24 active duty and 8 reserve VP squadrons covering deployments across the world. A squadron was designed to be support itself for long periods and be able to shift ASW operations to distant bases within a matter of hours.

Sonobuoys and Plot Stab(ilization) At KEF we flew a *"high mission"* and dropped sonobuoys from somewhere around 14,000 to 16,000 feet. When the sonobuoys hit the water, a string with a hydrophone deployed to pre-set depths. The buoys could be set for 1, 3 or 8 hours life (and then sank) and our sonar operators listened and recorded potential submarine signatures passively, so the sub didn't know we were onto them. It took quite a while for the buoys to drop and we often had problems with them freezing up on the way down, so it could be a crap shoot if they would come up and by then valuable minutes had been lost. We were constantly marking on top of a buoy to maintain plot stabilization so that we knew where the buoy pattern was in order to track a Soviet sub accurately.

Weather Big storms, winds, and changing weather routinely hit Iceland, so taxiing and taking off could be challenging in high gusting winds and icy concrete. KEF was notorious for quickly changing weather and heavy winds so our linesmen often tied themselves to the *"Buddha"* (big push-back tractor) to keep them from being blown into the propellers. One night, one of our planes ground-looped (was turned around into the wind) while taxiing out in high gusting winds on an icy taxiway. Sven, KEF's *"Snow King,"* led a crew who used big brushes and plows to keep the runway constantly open in the teeth of winter. White-outs were a threat, especially in the dark of winter, so we had to be careful not to get disoriented and lost in blowing snow.

"Magic Power Levers" Keflavik was reporting deteriorating weather with winds gusting more than 30 knots at over 30 degrees off the runway, light turbulence, and blowing snow as the PPC (Patrol Plane Commander) and I were briefing his night approach after our 8-hour patrol when he said *"You take it."*

As the GCA (Ground Controlled Approach) controller talked us onto glide path; I kept telling myself "Concentrate, stay on the gauges, smooth power changes, don't peek outside, keep scan going" and made tiny corrections with the rudder pedals according to the commands of the controller, who set us up crabbing into the wind down the bumpy approach.

The windshield wipers going high speed made a thumping urgent sound and close to approach minimums we broke out of the clag and I transitioned outside to dazzling driving snow shooting past in the landing lights and saw the approach and runway lights shining up in the night. I fought to stay aligned on centerline compensating with crosswind corrections with wing-down and top rudder and flared to land smoothly—which was a very big mistake-- because the runway was slick and suddenly we were sliding sideways off centerline, but quickly, the 4 power levers started moving magically in my right hand as the PPC applied asymmetric thrust to correct to centerline and compensate for my mistakes. I had maybe 350 flight hours total, my knees were shaking, but the lessons from this experience remained imprinted on me. Months later, returning from our final mission on the deployment, I landed firmly in driving rain and gusting crosswinds and was able to maintain control as we started to hydroplane (at something like your speed about 9 X the square root of your tire pressure) on the standing water.

When finally qualified after years of training, your Patrol Plane Commander papers said you were qualified **"to take the P-3C and crew anywhere in the world in any weather"** which was quite a commission and responsibility. Our Royal Air Force exchange Squadron Leader pilot said **"I was initially shocked to see that you had Lieutenants Junior Grades (about 25 years old) as crew-holding PPCs, but later I saw that they performed very well."**

The "Tube" (fuselage) was dominated by many feet of the *Univac CP-901* digital computer with blinking lights mounted in bays along the port side. The TACCO (Naval Flight Officer-NFO Tactical Coordinator) managed the tactical picture via the new computer system and had a large 15" round display, a keyboard, a *track ball* roughly the size of an orange (which was an early *mouse*), and a lot of push-buttons; we had a smaller tactical display in the cockpit. NAVCOMs (NFO Navigator Communicators) carefully monitored and updated the inertial navigation system (INS) to maintain aircraft position and sonobuoy plot stabilization. The NAVCOMs also spent a lot of effort trying to perfect new data link communications systems.

Due to the P-3C seating arrangement, crews had to learn to communicate briefly and effectively via the Intercom; some TACCOs used long lead cords to be able to walk back to see sensor displays and talk with the operators. Eventually our Sensor Operators were trained in something very new--plasma touch screens--to help them process acoustic data quicker.

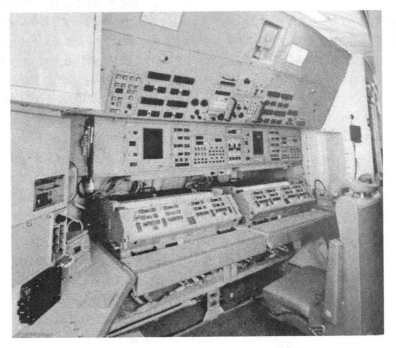

Acoustic Sensor SS1 & SS2 stations *US Navy*

CP-901 (Univac 1830A) Computer In 1962 Naval Air Development Center (NADC) created a concept for a new digital airborne computer *(called ANEW)* to upgrade patrol capabilities. Sperry-Rand's Univac Defense Systems Division worked on developing a prototype and initially looked at integrated circuits used for the USAF Titan II inertial guidance system, but decided to build a new computer which was compatible with NTDS; in 1963 they provided the CP-823U prototype to NADC. In 1966 the Navy contracted with Univac to work with NADC on a Navy contract to **coordinate airborne patrol sensors (acoustic and non-acoustic: radar, MAD, infrared, etc.)** and utilize the new **Naval Tactical Data System (NTDS).** In 1968 this effort evolved into the first airborne digital ASW computer CP-901 /ASQ-114 computer using 30-bit Instruction Set Architecture[110] which formed the avionics backbone of the top-of the line P-3Cs flown by NAS Jacksonville squadrons which I flew as I joined VP-45 in 1976.

The IFT (Inflight Technician) was a new and vital position on P-3C crews to keep the moody CP-901 computer and avionics going. **The CP-901 was notorious for dying just at the wrong time, like during the run-in for an attack and mad trapping to maintain contact.** It took a good crew to quickly transition to manual tracking when the CP-901 died. Another overall problem at JAX was that the priority for avionics parts went to deployed squadrons and sometimes key parts for the avionics suite were unavailable to keep all the aircraft up to ASW readiness.

*AVCM (Ret.) Jim Cole, our Combat Air Crew (CAC) 2 IFT says:

> *"I have **5-10 times the computing power in my iPhone 6** than was in the man-sized CP-901...After getting a hot contact in ASW, it was very rare for a crew of a P-2 or a P-3A/B to still have contact when going OFSTA (Off Station). The opposite was true of the P-3C. When it got a sniff, with a competent crew, it hung*

---

[110] Rapinac J, Blixt B. 2006 VIP Club Information Technology Pioneers, http://vipclubmn.org/sysairborne.html *A History of the Relationship between Sperry Univac Defense Systems Division and Lockheed California Aircraft Company; P-3C Early Computer Development at Univac; 30-Bit Computers Chapter,* Information technology Pioneers, http://vipclubmn.org/CP30bit.html

*on. I remember a Fleet exercise we participated in VP-56, where our services were declined, so we were kept high and out of the way of the fleet's S-2s and helos. With our sensors, we were able to watch the enemy sub (one of our own actually), sneak in through the escorts, and sink (stimulated) the task force's carrier, while the players on the surface hadn't a clue. **The (P-3) "Charlie", was such a quantum leap in ASW - I don't think we'll ever see another leap like that in weapon systems again.** I, like Admiral Tobin, feel really good about the sub-hunting we did, especially in the late Seventies, early Eighties."*

***AVCM Jim Cole grew up in Ipswich Massachusetts and retired out of VA-105 at NAS Cecil Field after 20 years in the Navy. He spent over thirteen years at NADEP JAX, majority of the time working as part of the TMCFA team for P-3 Tech Pubs and is retired in Jacksonville FL.

CP-901 computer IFT station (note bench seats in equipment bay which I rode from JAX to Iceland as a New Guy)

IFT Jim Cole *VP-45 1977 Cruisebook*

We carried 84 sonobuoys: 36 internals and 48 externally mounted in the belly; the buoys could be set for 1, 3, or 8 hours life. Each TACCO had different buoy deployment tendencies; for example, when LT Stump.... started to lose contact, he would let loose what he called a ***"rain of steel"*** (many buoys) to try to regain contact. I think buoys cost about $100 each for the common LOFAR and about $500 for a DIFAR. Ordnancemen called the aircraft belly sonobuoy tube area *Sherwood Forest* because when you looked up, the many tubes resembled trees.

Hazards on Patrol Since we usually operated in EMCON (Emissions Control--all transmitters and other active emitters turned off) on 8 to 10 hour-long missions often 2-3 hours from base, if something happened, you were on your own. Monitoring activities might not know that you were missing until you failed to return at the end of an on-station period which might delay Search And Rescue (SAR) efforts for several hours. We operated with forecast barometric altimeter settings which could be somewhat inaccurate and this could be a big problem--especially at night when you were descending IFR (on instruments) below 1000 ft.

*Jim Cole recalled that,

"On one patrol out of Iceland, our TACCO and Sensor operators determined that a sonar convergence zone condition existed and

*that we should hop over 100 miles east towards Europe to lay more sonobuoys to catch the sub. As we were putting the pattern in, an Aft Observer suddenly told the pilots that they **saw an RAF Nimrod also laying buoys in the same area**—which was a very big problem—having two ASW aircraft in the same area— neither having been briefed about the other."*

P-3 Magnetic Anomaly Detection (MAD) For practice attacks using MAD, you might descend in the middle of the night with poor visibility to 300 feet using a several hours-old forecast barometric altimeter setting, so you needed to transition carefully trying to maintain some sort of visual horizon—and if you were IFR, it could be a tense time. Flying a clover leaf MAD pattern required thinking ahead and a smooth set of hands. You pulled slight G as the bank angle increased and kept an eye on the horizon and MAD-trapped at 200 feet in the day and 300 feet at night; The goal was to get quickly back around on top of a submarine to enable the Sensor 3 Non-acoustic operator to get a MAD needle swing to pinpoint the target and enable the TACCO to attack.

Amateur IFT On a VP-49 mission, our On Top Position Indicator (OTPI) died just when we were tracking a Russian nuke in the middle of the Atlantic; our IFT tried to fix it, but we had to abort- -losing contact-- and request immediate launch of the ready crew which was over 2 hours away.

I was so pissed-off that I got out of the seat and went back and talked with our IFT. I unbolted the OTPI and asked him he had drop-tested it on the deck mat like this? (yes); had he put illegal Freon on the connections like this? (yes); had he thrown it into the freezer like this for 10 minutes to re-scramble the electrons? (yes). So, I got a cup of coffee, took the OTPI out of the freezer, dropped it on the deck again, slammed it backed into its compartment, and went back to the galley when I heard Flight yell over the PA "the OTPI is working!" So, we worked to regain our Plot Stab and regained contact and told the enroute Ready crew that we were back in contact!

Mail for Jan Mayen On one patrol, we were also asked to try to drop the mail (in a sonobuoy) to the Norwegians manning the isolated LORAN site on a tiny island north of the Arctic Circle. The Norwegians hadn't gotten mail for many weeks and it was now January. The TACCO reported winds gusting to 70 knots (of course blowing us toward the cliffs) but the Norwegians claimed the winds were only 25 knots or so. The PPC made a couple of attempts and eventually dropped the mail on the icy beach at 200 feet in a wild gusty approach. As we departed, the Norwegians said *"Thanks very much for dropping our mail—we haven't had mail since before Christmas; and no one has ever been able to drop before in 70 knots of wind!"*

*IFT Jim Cole recalls that flight:

"I remember one particular Jan Mayen mail-drop (not one of my favorite flights, by the way), where we came in for the drop, all was smooth until we came over that small plain and got behind the tops of the mountain ridge. The wind was 'roiling' so bad over that ridge, that it flipped us over the 90 before we knew it. The cockpit had a heck of a fight, from what I'd heard. I was doing the duty at the door, in the old parachute harness secured to the deck D rings & I swear I saw horizon past the toes of my flight boots near bottom edge of the door. That part of the memory is very vivid"

Detachments The squadron sent crews to augment bases whose Op Areas were overloaded with Soviet submarine activities. Crews periodically were assigned bases such as Bodo Norway and Lajes in the Azores to assist.

One day in KEF, the squadron was sent a short-notice tasking to quickly **send a crew from Iceland back to NAS Norfolk, Virginia to load-up practice torpedoes and then drop them in an exercise off the East Coast.** I think the crew may have been one of our two Ready Alert crews and their long-flying on the torpedo exercise showed our abilities to transition quickly to a wartime posture and carry out operational orders.

Nicknames A crew took off from KEF for a *"Good Deal"* 3 day stay at the NATO base in Bodo, Norway. The PPC made the takeoff, got to top of climb, went back to sleep in the rest racks in the back. He woke up as the plane started descending and sat on the radar console for the approach. *"This place has a lot of WWII Hangars and snow just like KEF; Hey, look there are some of our P-3s here, too."* What the PPC didn't know was they had had a mechanical failure and returned to KEF--but he didn't figure it out until the crew landed, so he instantly became *"Geographic Jack."*

A new officer had just checked into the squadron and he introduced himself at a squadron party as *"I'm Robert-don't call me Bob"* so for 3 years he was *Robert-don't call me Bob.* Every time someone mentioned a foreign place they had been, a new guy NFO said "I've been there," so he soon became *BenThere.* When M(ike) Olenick checked onboard, of course it didn't take long for him to become *"the Mole."*

Aerospace Rescue and Recovery Service *USAF*

*USAF HC-130 Rescue Alerts at KEF My retired Air force friend, LtCol Steve Walsworth remembers being TDY (Temporary Duty assignment) at KEF for Christmas 1976 as a junior pilot at RAF Woodbridge England:

*"We did 24/7 alerts for COMICEDEFOR. The evening that we got in was the only night we could drink so we'd try to make the most of it at the O' Club on that night. Ran into some P-3 guys there and they invited us to the **Brass Nut. Loved the jukebox with the inverted P3 flying over the carrier picture on it.** We only needed 3 rooms, but Navy let us have 1 for a day room. Since we were from the 67th ARRS (Air Rescue and Recovery Service) the day room got named the "ARRS Hole. The floor above us was "the Bone Yard boys"--nickname we gave the EC-121 guys because their planes were going to DM (Davis Monthan AFB Tucson AZ) & getting replaced with AWACS."*

*I remember one time the Jolly (HH-3) had just plugged into our (refueling) drogue and called "contact" and still had the mike keyed when he had a **Chips Light come on** and continued with "... Oh s--t!" Chips-light in helios is a Land Now! maneuver. Trouble was, we were over water about 3 miles off the coast. All we heard was the "contact...oh s--t" and felt the helio unplug. "*

***LtCol Steve Walsworth graduated from San Jose State University and was commissioned through Air Force ROTC in 1973. He graduated from Air Force pilot training in 1974 and went to advanced Aerospace Rescue and Recovery Service (ARRS) training. Steve was later stationed at RAF Woodbridge, UK and assigned to the 67th ARRS Squadron from 1976-1979 when he flew missions out of Keflavik, Iceland. He retired from the Air Force after 23 1/2 years with almost 5,000 hours of flight time and 5 rescue saves. He later flew for Vanguard Airlines and FedEx, retiring in 2011 after a 39-year aviation career.

*On my 1971 Midshipman summer cruise aboard the carrier USS Franklin D. Roosevelt (CVA-42) I begged a ride on an SH-3 helo. The AC let me ride in the left seat as we delivered mail, etc. He said "just watch the annunciator panel and tell me if any lights go on." We were hovering and lowering the chaplain onto a destroyer when I saw a light come on and so I said quietly "GEARBOX CHIPS." He said "S---" and suddenly he let the chaplain down very fast and we pulled off and went down skimming the ocean all

the way back to the Wasp; I was trying to read the escape door instructions next to me.

SAR (Search And Rescue) One day a civilian pilot ferrying a single-engine plane across the North Atlantic called "Mayday" as he ditched well south of Iceland due to engine failure; KEF launched the SAR helicopter and found the pilot sitting on top of his canopy and rescued him! Another time a HC-130 and HH-3 worked to heroically rescued a very sick sailor from a submarine in the Atlantic.

The Air Force had a few EC-121s (Lockheed *Constellations*) and a squadron of F-4 interceptors, the *Checkertails*, at KEF. The fighters were on constant alert so the pilots had bricks (walkie talkies) with them; they also wore black and white checked ascots with their flight suits, shined their flight boots (we tried not to shine ours too much because someone had told us in flight school that too much shoe polish was a fire hazard), and had their own BOQ bar called the Whiff(enpoof?) which was not the *'Nut* by a long shot. One day an Air Force pilot yelled *"Dead Bug"* (an Air Force tradition) and everyone hit the deck (floor) on their back with their legs up—the last one on their back had to buy the beer. Unfortunately, someone knocked a fighter pilot off his bar stool and he broke his elbow, so the *Checkertails* had one less interceptor pilot. What do you think the Air Force did about this? True to form, they painted a red line around a corner of the bar room to be the *"Designated Dead Bug Area."*

Chapter 14
Bermuda, Training, Sigonella
(SIG) Sicily, and Navigation

Why the Radar Range Knob is Really VERY Important In 1979 a couple of VP-45 crews were sent from to NAS Bermuda for a week-plus to augment the Brunswick squadron deployed there to fly on a surge of Russian *Yankee* missile boats.

*It was a great chance to fly an operational patrol against Soviet subs almost every day and stay off-base at a beach hotel. It was late winter and the weather was pretty bad. One day our crew took off into the overcast and as usual set EMCON. We had a rough ride and as we got closer to on station east of Bermuda, I asked the Sensor 3 (a senior replacement who was just flying with us on this flight to get monthly flight pay) to break EMCON, take a couple of sweeps on the radar to make sure we would be OK on station. He said that it looked good and a couple of **minutes later we started picking up heavy rain, then heavy hail, moderate turbulence, lightning and St. Elmo's fire, then severe turbulence and we were headed down. I pushed up Max Military power and tried to keep the wings level, but we were still descending rapidly and the plane was trying to roll over**—I had never experienced anything like it. The co-pilot was helping me and yelling "Keep the wings level" and calling off altitudes, but we were at the mercy of the huge cumulonimbus we had flown into. Finally, the downdraft spit us out around 2,000 feet and I recovered—you could see the heavy hail being spit out the downdraft of the CB.*

We checked to see that everyone was OK and put a ring of buoys in around the base of the CB where, of course, according to Murphy's law, the Yankee was below. I asked the TACCO what the heck had gone wrong with the radar and he reported that the replacement Sensor 3 had taken a look ahead with the range scale set so far out that he only saw clutter in front of us—that almost killed 12 crewmen. The rugged P-3C had saved us riding down the downdraft within the shaft of a probably 40,000 foot-plus CB; we had managed to survive **before windshear recovery procedures were written.** *DCS*

One of the Very Best: CDR R.F. Stephenson USN *US Navy*

"Shaft Horsepower 700" Our new XO, CDR Bob Stephenson, checked into the squadron and he was a pilot's pilot. Bob had been a Machinist Mate, went to Pensacola as a NAVCAD, and had a load of flight experience including flying C-47s and other aircraft in Vietnam. He flew over to Bermuda to see how our detachment was doing flying on a surge of Russian *Yankee* missile boats and flew back with us to JAX. About an hour out of JAX, he started talking about "one power setting landings" and whether it could actually be done and then bet me a beer that he could do it. So, during the descent at about 12,000 feet he said *"Set Horsepower 700."* I knew he couldn't make Runway 9 since he was still high as a kite at about 3,000 feet at the right 180. We were still about 1500 feet turning on final and I knew he couldn't get it down, but Bob calmly said *"Ask for a left 360."* I did and couldn't believe that JAX tower approved it and Bob greased it on perfectly. ...he was the real deal.

Balancing a Zippo *We spent a lot of time bouncing (doing touch and go practice landings) and instructing in the pattern at the NS Mayport field; in the late '70s, the coast and Amelia Island had not been developed yet. An Instructor Flight Engineer bet me I couldn't land and reverse without tipping over his Zippo lighter (people smoked in back then) which he put sideways (not fore and aft) on the fuel totalizer glass gage (I won).*

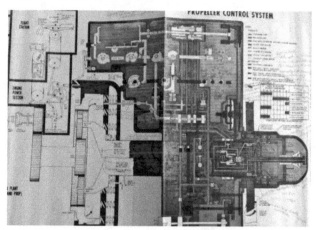

Prop Diagram from the P-3C NATOPS *(The Blue Sleeping Pill)*
"What does that Reverse Back-up Valve do? Explain the flow of prop fluid from the reservoir and how the prop works.." DCS Photo

Puke-us The P-3 Navy had embarked on a new "PQS" system (Personal Qualification System known locally as *Puke-us*) and we had to get extensive sign-offs for each qualification: 3P, 2P, PPC. At KEF I often tried to pester PPCs to get PQS sign-offs and many of them would run away trying not to spill their beers when they saw me coming to avoid *Puke-us* discussions on fun things like how the "reverse back-up valve" worked in the complex prop diagram.

NAF Sigonella (SIG) is located south of Mt. Etna and west of Catania and been a WWII base and in the late 1970s you could still see the "lollipops" of tarmac (with concrete poured around them later) where Italian and German fighters had been positioned. At SIG Naval Air Facility (NAF) II, we got to see their **F-104 fighters**

and Breguet *Atlantic* twin engine patrol planes training and operating. We heard that the Italian Navy practiced *real* single engine landings with an engine actually shut down (we only pulled the engine back to idle) and even had wine in their inflight meals.

Gulf of Hammamet & Sicily *wikipedia/commons*

SIG was a low altitude mission and we flew around the Med usually at 1500 or 2500 feet on the hunt for mostly diesel submarines and almost every mission had a "Ham(mamet Bay off Tunisia) Check" to photo the Soviet wagon wheel of ships and subs. A typical SIG mission involved **shutting down #1 engine at Top of Climb, transiting to on-station, shutting down #4 and loitering on patrol search**; if descending below 2500 feet you had to relight off #4 and if you went below 1,000 feet you lit off #1 engine. Sonar ranges were very short due to the shallowness of the Med, mud bottom in places, etc.

*TACCO Warren Tisdale remembers:

"Sigonella operations were a lot different from those in Keflavik. There was considerably less long-term tracking of submarines

*with hot turnovers to relieving aircraft. Mostly short contact and a lot of surface search/reconnaissance. The missions were more helter-skelter, with an anchorage check either going out or coming in, or both. **Rigging ships at Hammamet (Tunisia) and Kythira (Greece) anchorages, with the occasional puckering flight near Sollum (Egypt).** Short detachments to Souda Bay, Crete. **Low level and bumpy flights with a lot of surface traffic.** One night we jumped a sub that was submerging right as we roared into Hammamet. We rained down buoys—but were not able to track it because we couldn't identify the sub's acoustic signature amongst all the noise."*

TACCO LTJG Warren Tisdale *VP-45 1977 Cruisebook*

***LT Warren Tisdale graduated from Davidson College in 1974, taught high school Algebra, and was commissioned through AOCS in 1975, joining VP-45 in February 1977 on the KEF deployment. He also deployed to SIG twice, was TACCO NATOPS, and left the squadron and the Navy in 1980 after his 3 ½ year commitment post NFO Wings. Warren graduated from Duke Law School in 1983 and has been a career environmental law and land use attorney in Norfolk.

Diesel Submarines At the end of WWII, the US and USSR

competed to capture German engineers, scientists, and technology. The Russians acquired German diesel submarine technology and improved electric battery designs and developed the *Whiskey, Foxtrot, Juliett,* classes of diesel submarines.

Night-hunting the *Juliett* We flew at lower altitudes to enable use of all sensors: radar, sonar, FLIR (infrared), and our observers' eyes. Our Ops Officer worked out a set of innovative tactics for crews to hunt the *Juliett* on many nights. The *Juliett* was a big conventional diesel boat with 4 nuclear-capable cruise missiles with a range of 300 miles which threatened our Carrier Battle Groups in the Med. Since they had to snorkel or surface at night to keep their batteries charged up, Ops set up a nightly plan to hunt the Juliet using over the shoulder radar and coordinating observers to scan up-moon. On an 8-9 hour patrol, the TACCO set up a watch schedule to rotate aft observers frequently because their **Recognition Differential ("RD")** ability to alertly scan the ocean) declined rapidly after 15 or 20 minutes, especially in the middle of the night.

1985 My crew on a *Foxtrot* (crew 78, 15 kts submerged) in the Med.
Ltjg Kevin Prindle USN

We often flew at low altitudes at night on three engines to loiter and conserve fuel.

*We kept the curtain to the flight station tightly closed and the red instrument lights turned way down to **keep our night vision peaked** so that we could see and possibly find a submarine* *snorkel or sail in the dark expanse. If you were really tired, the glow from the red instrument lights might seem to pulsate. We* **kept an eye on each other** *to make sure no one was bobbing in his inertial harness, nodding off. You leaned as far forward toward the windshield as possible to try to make out a vague horizon on the dark expanse of the Mediterranean which blended into the surface haze. You had the feeling of smallness and aloneness looking into infinity with not much to focus on. Although the* **Flight Engineer's cigarettes** *probably didn't help our night vision much, their pungent smell wafting around did help keep us awake...and you kept drinking coffee to keep going. The Navy drank black coffee, but I was one of the very few who added cream and sugar which made me the object of derision: "2 black coffees and a milkshake for Mr. Stanton..."*

You kept up chatter on the Intercom to see who was awake, talking with the TACCO about the prosecution plan and **Sensor 3—the main star of the radar hunt for the Juliett** *charging its batteries—***and the Aft Observers.** *It was a tiring business, flying patterns at night with radar looking over your shoulder and peering out into the dark in hopes of seeing a snorkeling Juliett missile sub.*

While the monotony, the dust, and months of being deployed to Sigonella gradually wore crews down, hearing Sensor 3 yell: "Small radar contact-could be sub sail--bearing 065..." instantly perked everyone up. The Plane Commander would swing the plane around quickly, yelling **"Light-off Number 1 (Engine)"** *and then after it spooled up,* **"TIT (turbine inlet temperature) 1010"** *and the crew would drop down below 1000 feet, running up the bearing... the hunt to localize and attack the Juliett sub was on."*

I constantly flew with a Low Altitude chart open on my lap so I could take ADF fixes and back-up the NAV; *it wasn't that I didn't trust him, but those old inertials had a tendency to drift and we were flying down-low a lot out of SIG. There were a lot small islands, towers, oil platforms etc. and it was good to know* *where you were especially if you were skirting land or islands. People think of the Mediterranean as having beautiful weather and beaches, but especially in the winter, there was bad weather. Sciroccos blew in from North Africa in the Spring and Fall and riled up the Med which was shallow and created very rough seas.*

One night we flew out of SIG at night during miserable weather with a lot of thunderstorms, lightning, and turbulence. The Sensor 3 reported strange intense radar echoes. We just managed to visually pick-out water spouts which seemed to be sprouting and snaking from the bottoms of clouds, so we carefully picked our away around these areas to avoid them.

Another night before dawn, I saw a red and green light of an aircraft coming toward us so I banked away a bit, but it continued on a constant bearing. I asked others to verify what they saw and we all agreed it was still coming at us. It turned out to be Venus refracting through the pre-dawn haze.

A former CO of Sigonella, Captain Tim Davison USN (Ret.) recalls that, "*NAF I near Motta Sant'Anastasia was actually a Luftwaffe weapons depot (using the train station collocated on Strada Stale 192 (SS-192) to deliver ordnance for the German fighters that flew out of the **20 some operational fields in the area.**"*

All VP-ers remember that Italian GCA controllers would talk you onto the glide path and then say *"Don't-a-toucha nuthin"* and if you slipped off glide path, you would hear *"You are now below glide path--I told you, don't a touch a nuthin..."*

*TACCO Warren Tisdale remembers:

*"SIG was hot with a lot of flies...Big flies that were not easily dissuaded. The locals were great; except for the guy hired to chip concrete off the forms used in the BOQ expansion project. He hammered rhythmically all day every weekday, which wasn't too bad unless you had flown all night and were trying to sleep, which was about 50 percent of the time. **Some boredom, some anxiety, some fear and some excitement on some flights.** Nice views of lava on Mt. Etna sometimes when flying back in at night.*

Changing topics, the TORPEX (Torpedo Exercise) training flights were great. We dropped a lot of electronic sonobuoys and electronic torpedoes on electronic submarines in the Weapons Systems Trainers. We occasionally tracked Soviet submarines in the wild, and worked with US submarines in exercises and coordinated ops. The torpedo flights however took you from the soup to nuts of real world ASW. Flying against a US submarine at the AUTEC range, with the sub using sound augmentation (otherwise we could not track them—they were much quieter than the Soviet submarines). You could make the buoy progression from LOFAR to DIFAR to Active, and then, with bomb bay doors open at very low altitude, **when SS3 called "MADMAN" you released the MK 46 torpedo down-course—** *or what you had concluded was down-course.* **At the TACCO seat you could feel the "clunk" of the torpedo release.** *After the aircraft climbed out, the range officer could tell you the range and relative bearing between the sub and the torpedo at the drop, whether the MK 46 torpedo ran as designed, and most importantly whether it acquired the submarine; the latter was the equivalent of a kill. Flying back to JAX after a successful acquisition, you could tell your crew (and yourself)" Hey, this stuff works."*

Incidents at Sea Hammamet was the Soviet anchorage off Tunisia which was used by submarines and sub tenders; there were picket ships stationed outward- usually small ships like *Grishas*. The Soviet Navy also used anchorages including Kythira NW of Greece, "East of Crete," and Sollum near the Egypt-Libya Border. They operated extensively in the eastern Med using the port of Tartus, Syria and also worked in the Gulf of Sidra off Libya. *One day we were rigging a Grisha outside Hammamet when it started training and slewing its gun at us. This was illegal according to the US-Soviet Incidents at Sea (INCSEA) Agreement which allowed a ship to slew a gun for maintenance, but it wasn't supposed to both slew and train (aim) at us. The Grisha fired several flares at us and one went up between our Number 3 and 4 engines.*

When we got back to Sig and debriefed at the ASWOC, we reported the incident and said we wanted to file an *INCSEA* report. The Debriefing Officer didn't want to do the paperwork and said *"But the flare didn't hit you..."* and we said we were just lucky that it didn't--and so we did file a report...just another Cold War situation.

*Retired H-46 pilot and Merchant Marine Master Mike Murphy recalls:

*"Your incident with the flares and the INCSEA violation brought back an incident of my own--a Soviet flare up through my rotor system. It was never reported because I probably deserved it, but I had been directed to look for something specific on the 3 vessels we encountered. It was **in the Indian Ocean....one of them finally got tired of me and fired the flare through my rotor system**. Never a word from either side though. We had caught them with something..."*

Your memories of night instruments brought back night launches off of the back of ships where it looked like you just flew into a coal sack....instant transition from visual cues and trying not to hit the hangar to the meager instrument panel of the H-46 and trying not to fly into the water. Lots of great memories and still here to tell about it."

Mt. Etna erupted a few times on our SIG deployments. Since we were often downwind of the volcanic ash cloud, Maintenance had to **"walnut shell'** (run pulverized walnut shells) through the engines to clean the turbine blades to prevent them from corroding and weakening. Squadrons invested a great deal of time and effort on corrosion control of aircraft surfaces and engines; going through the "bird baths" at the end of each flight helped control corrosion. Due to efforts spent grinding out and repainting to control corrosion, some aircraft became very spotted and were sometimes called *"Leopards."*

Late 1970s Navy Pilot Shortage The largest airline hiring took place in the late 1970s as the airlines replenished their WWII era pilots. In 1976, I remember pilots getting 4-5 offers from different airlines and having to decide which one to join. This caused extreme pressure on the Navy to maintain their needs for training and squadron jobs. I think there were only about 50-some P-3 qualified LCDRs left in my year group 1972. In the early 1980s, the Navy did several things to build-up pilot manpower-- including a pilot retention bonus and a relaxation of the 20-20 vision requirement for pilot flight school applications. They also allowed NFOs to apply for pilot training and then return to the community where they came from. These newly-minted pilots transitioned from NFOs were called *"Transvest-FOs."*

*Going Home from the 1985-86 SIG deployment and the Mole's Air Force Education At the end of a SIG deployment, Ltjg Mole, VP-45's **Security Manager and a very junior NFO**, was given the high honor and distinction of being the last navigator out of SIG. Mole had to verify and burn the squadron's extraneous crypto allotment, so he went over to *the Fly Trap* (BOQ bar) and grabbed 2 "volunteers" (including me) to witness his destruction of many crypto remnants. Mole recalls:

*"As Security Manager, I had to accompany the squadron's pallets which included classified material back to the states via the USAF Military Airlift Command transport. **It is important to note that this plane was entirely dedicated to returning the Squadron's classified gear to JAX via Rota with only 2 passengers, Mole and a Yeoman.** The C-141 was to depart Sigonella and proceed to NAS Rota Spain for a layover. Mole made all arrangements to store the classified material pallet and highly classified material (briefcase handcuffed to wrist) at Naval Station Rota Spain for the evening. Upon arriving at the aircraft in SIG, he was told the plane had an "issue" & had to fly to Frankfurt Air Base for maintenance before heading to JAX.*

About an hour after takeoff, Mole went to the cockpit to see what was wrong with the aircraft. The pilot seat was empty, the copilot was looking at a chart trying to figure where the plane was and the Flight Engineer was reading. He asked the co-pilot what was wrong with the aircraft and was told the radar was acting up. Upon observing a normally operating radar presentation, he asked them for the real reason: it was that the 141 crew had spent *the previous night in Rota and **wanted to stay at Frankfurt with a better BOQ and food.** Mole explained the pain they caused since the pallet and brief cases needed very special classified storage off the aircraft. He was assured Frankfurt was alerted."*

*One day I had asked the Naval Station Rota Spain BOQ clerk if the 8 air conditioners on the second deck were for VIPs and he said "Sir, were not supposed to tell you all this, but those are for the Air Force C-141 MAC crews—they won't stay here without air conditioning."...and they wouldn't stay at the new Navy BOQ at Sig either; they had their priorities.

*"...Upon landing at Frankfurt, security personal with rifles met Mole and took him with his handcuffed-attached briefcase to a secure facility and removed the pallet for storage in a secure hanger. Early in the evening, Mole called the female co-pilot and asked when takeoff was scheduled for the next day. Although she provided an answer, the Mole would regret this the next day. The next morning, Mole went to the Secure hanger to check on the secure pallet. **It was gone--replaced by coffin. A ton of cruise boxes with at least Confidential material missing, on his watch.** A facility member finally showed up and stated the squadron pallet was moved to another area.*

Mole settled down on the "webbing" First Class (only class) seat. The plane captain (E-4) met him and said he was in trouble because he: Didn't formally check in at the terminal, had crossed the dreaded flight line security "Yellow Line," and finally, was told he could have been shot. The Aircraft Commander then proceeded to dress-down Mole for "breaking crew rest" for contacting his co-pilot and told him she could have declared broken crew rest and delayed the takeoff by 2 hours. The rest of the trip was uneventful, but Mole had learned a great deal about the Air Force and the importance of their crew rest."

***Mike Olenick was commissioned through Miami of Ohio Navy ROTC, served in VP-45, VP-30, VP-16, and Patrol Wing 11. After retiring from the Navy, he has worked for many years in the telecommunications industry.

*Major Norm Donovan recalls "Vintage 1969 P-3 Navigation in the North Atlantic:

"In 1969, I was a Canadian Navigator on exchange duties with VP-24 departing Patuxent River, Maryland for Lajes AFB, Azores. Flying 6 hours enroute to start a 6-month deployment was a new experience for me because the RCAF did not deploy an entire squadron for 6 months. VP-24 sent 6 aircraft and crews to Keflavik, Iceland and 3 aircraft and crews to Lajes.

My crew included 3 pilots, one of whom filled the position of pseudo-navigator; I was the TACCO who was the REAL Navigator. 0815 hours 25 June 1969 Airborne; wheels-up and the inertial (main navigation system) dumps--not a rare occurrence for the P-3B. When we reach altitude, I will attempt another alignment.

"Set Condition 5" Time to get to work; "Radar-TACCO; fire up the radar" The doppler has not locked-on, wind speed climbing to eternity--I've seen this before. "TACCO; Radar is hard-down, it will not load...TACCO-Flight; Forward TACAN is down, aft system is working. TACCO; The ADF is down as well."

***This is why we have Navigators!**; time to turn on the LORAN (Long-range radio navigation system) and take these pilots to Lajes. Oh tilt, LORAN is down and the alignment of the inertial has also failed. **Time to take stock of what is left:** AHRS (attitude and heading reference system) and Wet Compass, Sextant, Driftmeter, Pencil, Map, E-6B manual air computer, and (most importantly) **Superior Canadian Navigation Skills.** Been here before, but not since my days in the Lancaster.*

We press on; single-position Sun lines and drift observations every 15 minutes, and a multi-drift wind once an hour--much to the amazement of my American colleagues who had only read about these procedures in their Navigation ancient history books. 2 hours later, solid undercast and therefore, so much for using the driftmeter. I did attempt taking drifts on the cloud tops, but got inconsistent results.

*5 hours later and **not a fix since leaving North America,** I am sitting behind the pilot searching for Mount Pico (7,700-foot former volcano northwest of Lajes) using the **Mark 5 eye-ball**. The Co-pilot, who has been in contact with the crew ahead of us who have just landed--reports that Lajes is under a cloud deck, which is **20,000 feet thick**, and the weather is the pits. Looking down, I can see the cloud tops about 8000 feet below us.*

What, me worry? Man is not lost, just confused. *(In 1969 Lajes radar had very poor coverage to the west due to the mountains, one had to fly east to get picked-up at any great distance.) I am staring forward looking up at the beautiful blue sky, wishing that it were full of stars when I suddenly realized that I was looking at a quarter moon and it was at right angles to the sun. **Saved! We have a sun/moon fix.** To the sextant; I take three sun/moon fixes and to my delight they **fall within 10 miles of my DR** (Dead reckoning) position.*

*On schedule, Lajes radar picks us up and we make an uneventful arrival. The Maintenance Chief takes my list of gripes and cries. **My 3 very grateful pilots satisfy my liquid requirements for the rest of the evening."***

Chapter 15
The 1980s Cold War

President Reagan championed the development of the *Strategic Defense Initiative (SDI)* and the US and USSR both fielded **mobile Intermediate-Range missiles**. President Reagan and Secretary of the Navy John Lehman proactively sent carrier battle groups and other units closer to Soviet bases and the Soviets did the same-- surging missile submarines and ships closer to the US.

Within the US, the CIA, Department of Defense (DoD), and the State Department often had differing views of the nature of the Soviet threat. In some cases, the Defense and Intelligence communities pushed analyses that there were "bomber gaps, missile gaps, chemical weapons gaps" which justified increasing defense expenditures. During the Reagan Administration, the Department of Defense published an annual report titled *Soviet Military Power* which served to inform Congress and the public to justify increased military budget expansion.

This was a time of growing tensions and uncertainties as both superpowers developed more lethal nuclear capabilities and counter-measures. Both sides sought to learn what the others were thinking about strategic nuclear plans and tactics. Both sides engaged in intense **espionage activities.** One of the US' most valued sources was **Russian General Dimitri Polyakov**, an officer who had become disillusioned and scared by Soviet planning, became a long-term American asset in the early Sixties and **was executed in the Eighties after being exposed by the CIA traitor Aldridge Ames. Polyakov's accurate and timely information helped moderate and calm American views, especially in times of rising US-Soviet tensions during President Reagan's Administration.**

Eva Dillon observed: "The full effect of Polyakov's intelligence output in helping the United States manage the Cold War is, in retrospect, astonishing. By reading the candid thinking of the Soviet high command in Military Thought and other documents that Polyakov slipped to the Americans, **US military experts came to understand the Russians' assessment of nuclear war was not much different from their own.** This was not the Pentagon's judgement prior to the clarity provided by Polyakov's intelligence. 'Many believed,' wrote **Admiral William Crowe (head of the Joint Chiefs of Staff under President Reagan)**, who was leading the yearly American political/military special war games at the time, 'that the Soviets would use (nuclear weapons)—that was the American defense establishment's best judgement.'"

Eva Dillon notes that, "Polyakov's intelligence showed that Soviet military leaders were as worried as their American counterparts, that they were not, in fact, 'crazy warmongers.' This revelation that **'may have prevented US miscalculations that would have touched off a shooting war,' said Robert Gates (Director of CIA under President George W. Bush)**, and helped change American political-military doctrine in the latter years of the Cold War."

"The Soviet technology-gathering effort revealed by Polyakov was 'breathtaking' according to Richard Perle, Assistant Secretary of Defense for International Security (under President Reagan). 'We found there were 5,000 separate programs that were utilizing Western technology to build up their military capabilities.' The documentation Polyakov provided spurred the United States to severely tighten controls on Western military technology."[111]

CoCom During the early years of the Cold War, the US and Allies established the **Coordinating Committee for Multilateral Export Controls (CoCom)** to review and stop key western technologies from being exported to the Soviet Bloc. Throughout the Cold War, the Defense, Commerce, and State Departments worked on interagency efforts and collaborated with Allied counterparts to review export policies. CoCom was especially focused

---

[111] Eva Dillon, *Spies in the Family,* New York, Harper Collins Publishers, 2017, pp. 175-177

on technologies which could be used to improve nuclear weapons and guidance and there were there were ongoing pressures by Western companies to export technologies and manipulate CoCom regulations.

The 1980s Toshiba-Kongsberg case involved Japanese and Norwegian companies which illegally exported numerically controlled 9 axis milling machines to the Soviets enabling them to do more precise work in many defense industries. In the anti-submarine world we saw the results of the Soviets being able to machine smoother complex curves on submarine propellers—and suddenly, Russian submarines became much more silent and very difficult for us to track.

Even with these blatant examples, Western companies continuously sought relaxation of CoCom controls as the US and its Allies sought to solidify multi-national policies toward exports of critical technologies which could be used by the Soviet Bloc to improve weapons.

Arms Control Author John Newhouse writes that, "Its (nuclear arms control) purpose was—is—to make more remote the risk of nuclear war by reducing uncertainties and promoting stability. It is a political process...**Without the ABM treaty—the centerpiece agreement—there would be many more strategic weapons of all kinds. Without SALT II, the Soviets could have deployed a much larger force of their most threatening weapons—MIRV'ed ICBMs—than they did. And without some steady show of restraint, the superpowers will find it even harder to curb the traffic by other countries in weapons of mass destruction (WMD)."**[112]

Reykjavik Talks; the Beginning of the End President Reagan and Secretary Gorbachev met in **October 1986 in Reykjavik Iceland,** where Gorbachev surprised the US by proposing large nuclear weapons cuts, on-site inspections, and even human rights. **The optimism and momentum of Reykjavik provided a glimpse of the beginning of the coming end of the Cold War.**

Following up on Reykjavik, in December 1987 President Reagan and General Secretary Gorbachev signed the **Intermediate-Range**

---

[112] John Newhouse, Op. Cit., p. 421

Nuclear Forces (INF) Treaty which eliminated Intermediate and Short-range nuclear and conventional missiles and their mobile launchers. The INF treaty enabled each side to inspect the other's military facilities to verify the treaty's terms and initiated a period of confidence-building between the US and the USSR.

1986 Reykjavik Pres. Reagan and Sec. Gorbachev *White House Photo Office*

Conclusions

Over the 44 years of the Cold War, the US/Allies, and the USSR/ Warsaw Pact managed to **maintain military balance and stability at great costs** by building organizations of highly-trained professionals and the procedures to handle, support, maintain, and defend against nuclear weapons. While memories of the Cold War and those who served during it have faded, it is important that we look back at these critical times to study the crises, incidents, and lessons-learned and use them to form a baseline of knowledge as we toward tenser relations with our old adversaries.

Seeing the Cold war through Veterans' experiences helps to highlight the great challenges and costs to people and machines to maintain the relatively stable stand-off between the superpowers.

From 1947-1991, the Cold War dominated several generations as millions of American, NATO, Allied personnel and our professional counterparts in the Soviet Union, the Warsaw Pact, and China served in a myriad of positions which were vital to national defense efforts. The Cold War affected **not just those serving in the military and defense industries, but also had wide-ranging effects on families and communities.**

Looking back at the many incidents and crises of the Cold War, it is amazing that both the United States and the Soviet Union managed to stabilize their superpower stand-off and maintain controls to survive many complex events which had the potential to escalate into nuclear war. **It is a tribute to the professionals on both sides that a tense peace was maintained over forty dangerous years.**

It is important to review events of the Cold War so we can use **lessons-learned from past experiences** to assist in planning for future contingencies:

- Cherish Allies; build interoperability and cabilities to deploy quickly anywhere
- Create long-term regional and global alliances
- Plan an exit strategy before foreign intervention
- Do not encourage uprisings against regimes if you cannot support the consequences
- Learn more about adversaries, languages, and culture
- Build resilient Civil Defense programs
- Protect technologies and cyber activities

Many countries committed their blood and treasure to maintain peace and a balance of power during these turbulent and dangerous times; **we need to continue to remember their sacrifices, especially those still missing or lost at sea.**

From the last page of the *1977 VP-45 Cruisebook:*

"We were there. We were Patrol Squadron FORTY-FIVE. Four hundred individuals bound by a common goal; Freedom for all mankind. Those who have never faced the challenge...the reality...the loneliness will never understand. For who knows better the price of peace, than those who are willing to give their lives for it..."

Some Recommendations to Learn More about the Cold War:

- *Daring Young Men-The Heroism and Triumph of The Berlin Airlift June 1948-May 1949* Richard Reeves 2010
- **Korea - The Unknown War** PBS WGBH 1980
- **Korea - The Forgotten War** The History Channel 1987
- **Street Without Joy-The French Debacle in Indochina** Bernard B. Fall 1961
- **Hell in a Very Small Place-the Siege of Dien Bien** Bernard B. Fall 1966
- **Strategic Air Command** Jimmy Stewart 1955
- *Twelve Days-(Hungarian) Revolution 1956,* Victor Sebestyen 2007
- *Dr. Strangelove or: How I Learned to Stop Worrying and Love the Bomb* Peter Sellers, Slim Pickens 1964
- *The Bedford Incident,* Richard Widmark 1965
- *We Seven* by the Mercury Astronauts 1962
- *The Spy Who Came in from the Cold* John le Carré 1963
- **The Year of Living Dangerously** (about 1965 Indonesia) directed by Peter Weir from Christopher Koch's novel 1982
- *Vietnam-a History,* Stanley Kornow 1983
- **Chickenhawk** (Vietnam *Huey* pilot's memories) Robert Mason 1983
- **Six Silent Men** *Book Two,* Kenn Miller 1997
- **The Vietnam War,** film by Ken Burns and Lynn Novick, PBS 2017

- ***The Day After***, film by Edward Hume, directed by Nicholas Meyer, ABC TV Network 1983
- *War and Peace in the Nuclear Age,* John Newhouse 1988
- ***Blind Man's Bluff, The Untold Story of American Submarine Espionage,*** Sherry Sontag and Christopher Drew 1998
- ***Thirteen Days*** (film about the 1962 Cuban Missile Crisis) Roger Donaldson 2000
- *Berlin 1961-Kennedy, Khrushchev, and the Most Dangerous Place on Earth* Frederick Kempe 2011
- *Command and Control: Nuclear weapons, the Damascus accident, and the Illusion of safety,* Eric Schlosser 2013
- Cold War review https://www.ducksters.com/history/cold_war/summary.php
- ***By Any Means Necessary: America's Secret Air War in the Cold War,*** William E. Burrows 2001

Bibliography

Burrows W. (2001) *By Any Means Necessary: America's Secret Air War in the Cold War,* Farrar, Straus and Giroux, New York 2001

Churchill W. (1946) *Sinews of Peace* speech, March 5, 1946 at Westminster College, https://www.nationalchurchillmuseum. org/sinews-of-peace-iron-curtain-speech.html

Curry R. (2004) *Whispering Death; Our Journey With the Hmong in the Secret War for Laos,* iUniverse, Inc, Lincoln NE

Dead Hand-System Perimeter https://en.wikipedia.org/wiki/ Dead_Hand_(nuclear_war)

Donovan N. Canada, *VP International Book of Remembrance,* Accident List- United States http://www.vpinternational.ca/ BOR/US.html

President Eisenhower D. (1953), *The Chance for Peace Speech* to the *American Society of Newspaper Editors,* August 6, 2017, Washington DC.

President Eisenhower D. (1954), *State of the Union Address to Congress,* Washington DC

Ekiert G. and Kubik J. (2001), *Rebellious Civil Society : Popular Protest and Democratic Consolidation in Poland, 1989–1993,* University of Michigan Press, Ann Arbor

Engel J. (2017) *When the World Seemed New; George H.W. Bush and the End of the Cold War,* Houghton Mifflin Harcourt Publishing Co., New York

Gall C. (2017) *Iran Flexes in Afghanistan As US Presence Wanes, The New York Times,* August 6, 2017

Jampoler A. (2003) *The Rescue of Alfa Foxtrot 586,* Naval Institute Press, Annapolis *http://www.orneveien.org/adak/contributors/jampoler/*

Kempe F. (2011) *Berlin 1961-Kennedy, Khrushchev, and the Most Dangerous Place on Earth,* G. P. Putnam's Sons, New York

Knaus, C. (2017) *Australian Air Force put on alert after Russian long-range bombers heads south, The Guardian,* December 30, 2017

President Kennedy J. (1961) July 25th televised speech to the nation

Khrushchev S. (2000) *Nikita Khrushchev,* The Pennsylvania State University Press, University Park, Pennsylvania

McCullough D. (1992) *Truman,* New York, Simon & Schuster, New York

McGuiness B. (1997) *Coffee on the Wing Beam: Memories of the P2V Neptune,* Knights of the Red Branch Press, Clear Lake WA

Miller, K. (1997) *Six Silent Men Book Two,* Mass Market Paperback Ivy Books, New York

National Museum of American History http://americanhistory.si.edu/subs/const/anatomy/sovietsubs/index.html

Newhouse J. (1988) *War and Peace in the Nuclear Age,* Alfred A. Knopf, Inc., New York

Rapinac J, Blixt B. (2006) VIP Club Information Technology Pioneers, *A History of the Relationship between Sperry Univac Defense Systems Division and Lockheed California Aircraft Company; P-3C Early Computer Development at Univac;30-Bit Computers Chapter,* Information Technology Pioneers, http://vipclubmn.org/CP30bit.html

Reeves R. (2010) *Daring Young Men-The Heroism and Triumph of The Berlin Airlift June 1948-May 1949,* Simon & Schuster, New York

Schmitt E. (2017) US Troops Train in Eastern Europe to Echoes of the Cold War, August 6, 2017, *The New York Times*

Sebestyen V. (2007) *Twelve Days-(Hungarian) Revolution 1956,* Penguin Press, New York

Admiral Stavridis J. (2017) *Sea Power*, Penguin Press, New York

Stanton, D. (2017) *Hunting Soviet Submarines on a P-3C Crew*, US Naval Aviation Museum "Foundations" Journal, Pensacola http://www.navalaviationfoundation.org/namf/documents/Stanton%20-%20Hunting%20Soviet%20Submarines%20on%20a%20P-3C%20Crew%20-%20Fall%202017%20Foundation%20Magazine.pdf

Sontag S. and Drew C. (1998) *Blind Man's Bluff, The Untold Story of American Submarine Espionage,* PublicAffairs-Perseus Book Group, New York

Szewczyk M. (2005) *"Poznański czerwiec 1956"* Official figures

President Truman H. (1956) *Years of Trial and Hope-Memoirs*, Volume II, Time, Inc. Doubleday & Company, New York

Ulmann B. (2014) *AN/FSQ-7: the computer that shaped the Cold War.* de Gruyter Oldenbourg,

Zubok V. and Pleshkov C. (1997) *Inside the Kremlin's Cold War: from Stalin to Khrushchev,* Harvard University Press, Cambridge

CPSIA information can be obtained
at www.ICGtesting.com
Printed in the USA
FFHW02n1559221018
48938524-53165FF